THE CONRAN COOKBOOKS

ICED DELIGHTS

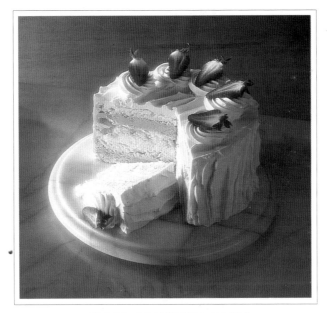

SHONA CRAWFORD POOLE

CONRAN OCTOPUS

First published in 1986 by
Conran Octopus Limited
28-32 Shelton Street
London WC2 9PH

Photographer Grant Symon
Editorial Consultant Caro Hobhouse
House Editor Susie Ward
Art Director Douglas Wilson
Art Editor Clive Hayball
Photographic Art Direction Valerie Wright Heneghan
Home Economist Elaine Bastable
Photographic Stylist Alison Williams
Art Assistant Nina Thomas

ISBN 1 85029 068 7

The publishers would like to thank the following
for their assistance with photographic props:
Heal's, 196 Tottenham Court Road, London W1;
The Conran Shop, Fulham Road, London SW3;
Habitat Designs Limited

Title page: Strawberry Ice Cream Cake (page 66).

Typeset by SX Composing, Essex
Printed and bound by Graficromo SA, Spain

CONTENTS

Real ices made with ripe fruit, fresh cream and natural flavours are a startling improvement on what most mass manufacturers call ice cream. The stuff they make with all those nameless fats, unpronounceable emulsifiers, numbered flavourings and coded colours is edible, but it is not the stuff of frozen dreams.

The chefs who run the finest restaurants make sorbets daily. The reason is not that they cannot make sufficient at once to last for a week or two, but because ices taste best fresh. For many cooks this is a counsel of perfection that will take second place to the convenience of having iced puddings on tap. But it is worth noticing the difference freshness makes.

Freezing in a sorbetière

If they have not already succumbed to ownership of an electric sorbetière which freezes and churns simultaneously, serious ice cream fanciers will be weighing up the cost against storage space and high-quality results.

It has to be said that ices made in the big sorbetières, or in the old fashioned hand-cranked churns, do have the smoothest, finest texture. This is due to the constant beating, of course, but also to the high speed at which they freeze – usually less than half an hour.

Electric freezer churns, the newest type of sorbetière designed for domestic use, are the most expensive. They are also the bulkiest machines, about the size of a heavy-duty typewriter, and quite a weight to lift. Against that, they make smooth ices quickly and efficiently. Models with a freezer bowl that can be removed for washing have an obvious advantage.

Hand-cranked churns requiring the addition of ice, salt and human motor-power make ices as smooth as those produced in electric freezer churns. And although they cost less than the newer models, they are not cheap.

Small electric sorbetières that churn the mixture inside your freezer – the rubber door seals accommodate the flex – are the least costly ice cream makers. In my experience the texture of the ices is not as smooth as that of ices made in the larger machines, nor is it a significant improvement on still-frozen ices. But if the convenience of forgetting the mixture once it is in the freezer counts, then one of these machines is worth considering. Best are models with paddles which automatically lift clear of the ice before it freezes hard.

Still-freezing

Still-freezing, as the term suggests, means freezing without simultaneously stirring. It simply involves using an ordinary container for the ice cream mixture and putting it in the freezer until it is firm. Most ice creams and sorbets need whisking or beating vigorously during the freezing process to break up the ice crystals, making the ice pleasantly smooth.

As a general rule, the richer or sweeter the recipe the less stirring or whisking it will need. Large flakes or crystals of ice form most readily in the least sweet or creamy ices, which must be taken out of the freezer and beaten to reduce the size of the ice crystals, at least once or twice during the freezing process.

The best possible time to beat any ice that does require whisking while it freezes is when the sides and bottom are almost firm and the centre is fairly liquid. The ice should be tipped into a chilled bowl and beaten really vigorously. This can also be done in a food processor, but it does not achieve quite the same aeriating effect as a well-timed beating. The whisked ice is then returned to the freezer to firm again. An overlooked ice that has frozen hard before beating is better softened in the refrigerator than at room temperature.

There are also plenty of ices in this book which can be frozen without any stirring at all, using any kind of freezer. Most of these are simple to make too, and most of them are either fairly sweet, or rich – or both – because sugar and fat are two ingredients which, like alcohol, inhibit the formation of large, gritty ice crystals. Another is gelatine, but its uses are limited in ice cream making.

When still-freezing, always turn the freezer to its coldest setting for at least an hour beforehand. The colder the temperature, the smaller the crystals of ice formed in the mixture. For the same reason, it helps to freeze ices in flat containers which are in direct contact with the freezing element. (Only the sorbets containing alcohol require a 4-star freezer or a freezer churn.)

Freezing times
Freezing times are so variable that even the vaguest instructions can be more misleading than helpful. One reason is that the relatively inefficient ice-making compartment of a small refrigerator will take much longer to do the job than a modern freezer working on its fast-freeze setting.

Containers affect freezing times too. Metal is a better conductor of cold than plastic, and a shallow metal tray in contact with the freezer element is the most efficient way to freeze any ice quickly.

The type of ingredients used also affects freezing times. Recipes with a high proportion of sugar or alcohol will generally take longest to freeze.

When still-freezing it may be wise to avoid the possible disappointment of half frozen ices by making them the day before they are needed.

Ripening
After a day or two in the freezer, most ices will be rock-hard and will require 'ripening' to show themselves at their best. Ripening or softening an ice to the consistency which makes the most of its flavour and texture should always be done slowly in the refrigerator – never hurried in a warm kitchen. The aim is to soften it enough to scoop and serve, or to eat and, as with freezing, timing will depend on the same factors.

Small quantities, individual servings or ices in flat containers will ripen more quickly than ices in deep containers or bombes. Small ices will need only 5 or 10 minutes. Bombes or big containers up to 30 minutes.

The sweetest and most alcoholic ices will tend to ripen fastest, and those from the most efficient freezers will take longer to ripen than those made in less cold ice-making compartments of small refrigerators.

Shona Crawford Poole

5

RHUBARB SORBET

Forced spring rhubarb first appears in the depths of winter and makes an unusual pale pink ice. The flavour is perfectly captured by baking the rhubarb with sugar and no added liquid.

—————— SERVES 6 ——————

1¼ lb (560 g) spring rhubarb
10 oz (275 g) caster sugar

Heat the oven to 350°F (180°C, gas mark 4).

Chop the rhubarb into short lengths and put it into a deep ovenproof dish with the sugar. Cover closely and bake for 45 minutes or until the rhubarb is very tender. Set it aside to cool.

Blend or process the fruit with its juice, or press it through a fine sieve to make a smooth purée.

Freeze in a sorbetière following the manufacturer's instructions. Or still-freeze (page 4), vigorously whisking the partially frozen ice at least once during the freezing process.

APPLE AND HONEY SORBET

This smooth apple sorbet is peachy-pink and intensely flavoured. Beware of overpowering the apple taste with a too highly scented honey. A hint of honey is lovely. Choose apples of character — whether eaters or cookers. Cox's orange pippins and Bramleys are good.

—————— SERVES 6 ——————

2 pints (1.2 litres) unsweetened apple juice
1½ lb (675 g) apples
6 oz (170 g) granulated sugar
2 tablespoons clear honey

Put the apple juice into a heavy saucepan, bring to the boil and simmer, uncovered, until reduced to about 1 pint (560 ml).

Peel, core and roughly chop the apples. Add the apples and sugar to the juice and cook gently until the apples are tender. Stir in the honey and set aside to cool.

Blend or process the apples to a smooth purée, or pass through a fine sieve.

Freeze in a sorbetière following the manufacturer's instructions. Or still-freeze (page 4), vigorously whisking the partially frozen ice at least once during the freezing process.

Left: Apple and Honey Sorbet, right: Rhubarb Sorbet.

Top: Seville Orange Sorbet, below: Pink Grapefruit and Mint Sorbet, left: Lime and Ginger Sorbet (page 10).

SEVILLE ORANGE SORBET

Capture the inimitable flavour of marmalade oranges during their brief new year season in this distinctive bitter orange sorbet. The ice is lightened with egg white, a technique which works best with strong flavours. Use the same recipe for the other sour citrus fruits — limes, lemons and grapefruit.
Because their peel is invariably eaten, Seville oranges are not treated with fungicidal wax. This means that they do not keep as well as treated citrus fruits and should be used as soon as possible.

―――――――― SERVES 6 ――――――――

1 lb (450 g) Seville oranges
8 oz (225 g) granulated sugar
¾ pint (420 ml) water
2 egg whites

Cut the peel from the oranges, using a very sharp knife, taking only a thin layer of zest and none of the pith.

Put the zest into a saucepan with the sugar and water and heat gently until the sugar has dissolved completely. Raise the heat and boil the syrup for 5 minutes, then set it aside to cool completely.

Squeeze the juice from the oranges and strain it. Strain the cooled syrup, then stir it into the orange juice.

To freeze in a sorbetière: lightly whisk the egg whites, combine them with the syrup, then freeze immediately, following the manufacturer's instructions.

To still-freeze (page 4): freeze the syrup to a heavy slush, then whisk the egg whites until they are stiff and beat them lightly into the partially frozen mixture. Freeze until the ice is a little firmer, then vigorously whisk once more for a really smooth sorbet. Return it to the freezer until it is firm.

PINK GRAPEFRUIT AND MINT SORBET

This is tart, refreshing and not too sweet. It could be served as a first course on a hot summer day.

―――――――― SERVES 6 ――――――――

3 large pink grapefruit
6 oz (170 g) caster sugar
½ pint (280 ml) water
4 tablespoons chopped fresh mint

Cut the peel from one of the grapefruit, using a very sharp knife, taking only a thin layer of zest and none of the pith.

Put the zest into a saucepan with the sugar and water and heat gently until the sugar has dissolved completely. Simmer the syrup for 5 minutes, then take it off the heat and stir in the mint. Set it aside until quite cold.

Squeeze the juice from all the grapefruit and strain it. Strain the cold syrup and stir it into the grapefruit juice.

Freeze in a sorbetière following the manufacturer's instructions. Or still-freeze (page 4), vigorously whisking the partially frozen ice at least once during the freezing process.

More chopped mint can be stirred into the partially frozen sorbet for a pretty, mintier effect.

LIME AND GREEN GINGER SORBET

Illustrated on page 8

Experiment to discover how much ginger you like in this tantalizingly hot and cold ice.

——————— SERVES 6 ———————

4 limes
1½-in (4-cm) cube fresh ginger root, sliced
8 oz (225 g) granulated sugar
¾ pint (420 ml) water
2 egg whites

Cut the peel from one of the limes, using a very sharp knife, taking only the zest and none of the pith.

Put the zest into a saucepan with the ginger, sugar and water. Heat gently until the sugar has dissolved completely, then simmer the syrup for 5 minutes. Set it aside for at least 12 hours to cool completely and infuse with the flavour of the ginger.

Squeeze the juice from all the limes and strain it. Strain the syrup, then stir it into the lime juice.

To freeze in a sorbetière: lightly whisk the egg whites, combine them with the syrup, then freeze immediately, following the manufacturer's instructions.

To still-freeze (page 4): freeze the syrup to a heavy slush, then whisk the egg whites until they are stiff and beat them lightly into the partially frozen mixture. Freeze until the ice is a little firmer, then vigorously whisk once more for a really smooth sorbet. Return it to the freezer until it is firm.

ICED PEARS

Fresh pears for filling should be shapely and slightly under-ripe. A potato peeler is a good tool for beginning to hollow out fruit and a teaspoon finishes the job neatly.

——————— SERVES 6 ———————

8 large, not too ripe pears
6 tablespoons fresh lemon juice
12 oz (340 g) granulated sugar
18 fl oz (500 ml) water

Cut the tops off all the pears, removing a lid of flesh with the stalk. Drop the lids into a large bowl of cold water acidulated with 1 tablespoon of the lemon juice to prevent the pears from discolouring. Hollow out the pears, leaving a shell about ¼ in (6 mm) thick. Put them into the acidulated water as soon as they are ready. Reserve the scooped-out flesh and cores.

Put the sugar and water into a large saucepan and heat gently until the sugar has dissolved completely. Raise the heat and boil the syrup for 2 minutes, then add the hollowed pears and the lids and bring the syrup back to the boil. Simmer for a further 2 minutes, then carefully remove the pears and lids from the syrup and drain on kitchen paper.

Choose the 6 best pears and lids and set them aside to cool. When they are quite cold set them on a sheet of baking parchment, levelling the bases if necessary to make them stand upright. Freeze them hard.

In the meantime, chop the 2 remaining hollowed pears and cook with the reserved pear flesh in the syrup until tender. Pass the fruit with the syrup through a fine sieve to make a smooth purée. Stir in the remaining lemon juice and leave to cool.

Freeze in a sorbetière following the manufacturer's instructions. Or still-freeze (page 4), vigorously whisking the mixture at least twice during the freezing process. While the ice is still soft enough to stir, use it to fill the prepared pear cases. Top with the lids and freeze again until firm.

Above: Iced Pears.

Top: Redcurrant Sorbet (page 16), right: Raspberry Sorbet, left: Gooseberry and Elderberry Sorbet.

RASPBERRY SORBET

Raspberries need no cooking to turn them into fresh-tasting sorbets. Both fresh and frozen berries are suitable for ices. This recipe can be used for a variety of other intensely flavoured soft fruits, including ripe strawberries, loganberries and mangoes.

———— SERVES 6 ————

1 lb (450 g) ripe raspberries, thawed if frozen
12 fl oz (340 ml) Basic Sorbet Syrup (page 78)
juice of 1 orange, strained

Rub the raspberries through a fine sieve to remove the pips, or process them briefly in a blender or food processor and strain the purée. Combine the purée with the syrup and orange juice. If you have time, chill the purée for 1-2 hours in the refrigerator before freezing it. This step allows the flavour to develop.

Freeze in a sorbetière following the manufacturer's instructions. Or still-freeze (page 4), vigorously whisking the partially frozen ice at least once during the freezing process.

GOOSEBERRY AND ELDERFLOWER SORBET

Even town rats can find elderflowers in municipal parks and cascading over the gas works wall in early summer when the first green gooseberries appear. Together they make a sorbet exotically perfumed like muscat grapes.

———— SERVES 6 ————

2 lb (900 g) green gooseberries
1 pint (560 ml) water
8 oz (225 g) granulated sugar
about 3 large elderflower heads

Wash the gooseberries (there is no need to top and tail them) and put them, whole, into a saucepan with the water. Simmer the fruit until it is tender, then strain the juice through a scalded jelly bag, or through a large sieve lined with a clean cloth. Knot the corners of the cloth and hang it until it stops dripping.

Tie the elderflower heads loosely in a piece of muslin and put them into a saucepan with the gooseberry juice and the sugar. Heat gently until the sugar has dissolved completely, bring to the boil, then cool immediately. By the time the syrup is quite cold, the elderflowers will have perfumed it strongly.

Discard the elderflowers and freeze the syrup in a sorbetière following the manufacturer's instructions. Or still-freeze (page 4), vigorously whisking the partially frozen mixture twice during the freezing process.

CARAMEL SORBET

This must be the simplest sorbet of all – just sugar, water and a dash of lemon juice.

———— SERVES 6 ————

12 oz (340 g) granulated or caster sugar
1½ pints (850 ml) water
juice of 1 lemon

Put the sugar and ¼ pint of the water into a heavy saucepan and heat gently until the sugar has dissolved completely. Wash down any sugar crystals from the sides of the pan with a pastry brush dipped in cold water.

Raise the heat and boil the syrup to a light caramel, no darker than a rich golden brown or the sorbet will be bitter instead of sweet. Immediately remove the saucepan from the heat and dip its base into cold water to stop the sugar from darkening still further.

Add the remaining 1¼ pints (700 ml) water to the caramel and leave it to dissolve and cool, stirring from time to time to hasten the process.

When the syrup is quite cold, stir in the lemon juice.

Freeze in a sorbetière following the manufacturer's instructions. Or still-freeze (page 4), vigorously whisking the partially frozen ice at least once during the freezing process. The more frequently it is beaten during freezing the smoother the sorbet will be.

CHOCOLATE SORBET

Because it has so much less fat than chocolate, cocoa is better for making this smooth, chocolate-flavoured sorbet.

———— SERVES 6 ————

12 oz (340 g) granulated sugar
18 fl oz (500 ml) water
vanilla extract
2 oz (50 g) cocoa

Put the sugar and water into a saucepan and heat gently until the sugar has dissolved completely. Raise the heat and boil the syrup for 1 minute, then remove from the heat and allow it to cool a little.

Stir a little of the syrup into the cocoa in a bowl, to make a smooth paste, then gradually stir in the remaining syrup.

Add vanilla extract to taste, remembering that the flavour of the finished ice will be dulled by freezing. Strain the mixture.

Freeze in a sorbetière following the manufacturer's instructions. Or still-freeze (page 4), vigorously whisking the partially frozen ice at least once during the freezing process.

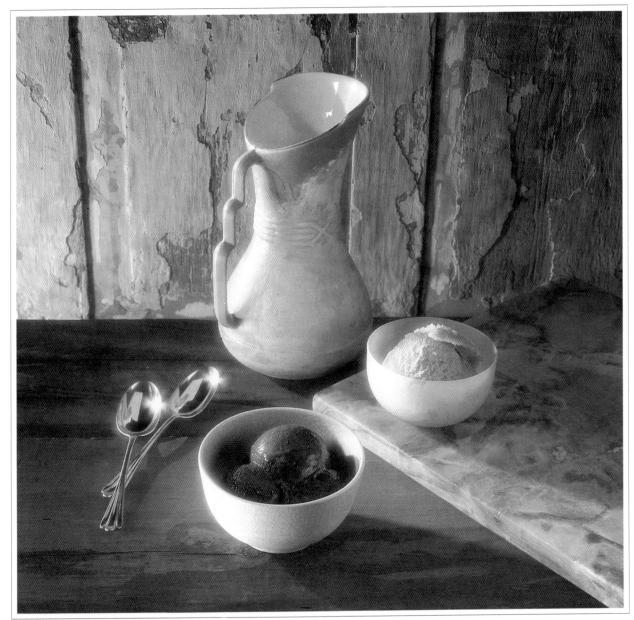

Left: Chocolate Sorbet, right: Caramel Sorbet.

REDCURRANT SORBET

Illustrated on page 12

The flavour of soft fruits like redcurrants and blackcurrants is enhanced by gently heating the fruit to extract the juice.

─────── SERVES 6 ───────

1½ lb (675 g) redcurrants
8 oz (225 g) caster sugar

Heat the oven to 350°F (180°C, gas mark 4).

Wash the redcurrants (there is no need to top and tail them) and shake off the excess water. Put them into a deep ovenproof dish with the sugar. Cover closely and bake for 30-45 minutes, or until the juices have run and the fruit is tender.

Pass the cooked redcurrants through a fine sieve to remove the skins, pips and stalks. Leave the juice to cool completely.

Freeze in a sorbetière following the manufacturer's instructions. Or still-freeze (page 4), vigorously whisking the partially frozen ice at least once during the freezing process.

CLARET GRANITA

Granitas are intentionally crunchy ices. An occasional, desultory stir — and no beating — during freezing is all that is required to produce the flaky crystals of ice that are their hallmark. Raspberries have an affinity with red wine which is shown to advantage in this ice.

─────── SERVES 6 ───────

4 oz (120 g) fresh or frozen raspberries, thawed if frozen
6 oz (170 g) granulated or caster sugar
4 fl oz (110 ml) water
1 bottle red Bordeaux wine

Mash the raspberries or process in a blender or food processor, then pass the pulp through a fine sieve to remove the pips. Set the purée aside.

Put the sugar and water into a small saucepan and heat gently until the sugar has dissolved completely. Raise the heat and boil the syrup for 5 minutes, then set it aside to cool.

When the syrup is quite cold, combine it with the raspberry purée and the wine.

To still-freeze: pour the mixture into a shallow, flat-bottomed container (preferably a metal tray, but a plastic box will also do) and freeze until the edges are firm and the centre of the ice is still liquid. Stir the sides to the centre with a fork, then return the mixture to the freezer until firm.

The same recipe frozen in a sorbetière to make a smooth ice is also delightful.

Above: Claret Granita.

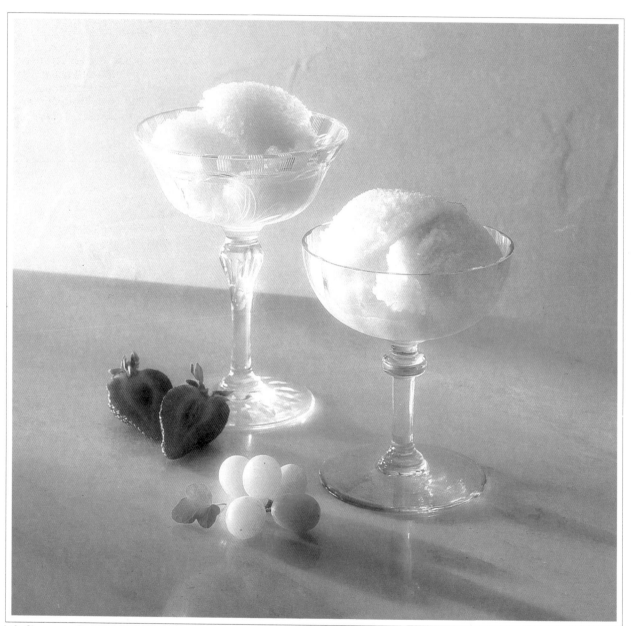

Left: Champagne Sorbet, right: Sorbet de Beaumes de Venise.

CHAMPAGNE SORBET

*Like champagne cocktails, champagne ices call for
nothing too grand in the way of wine and rely on other
ingredients for much of their flavour. Alcohol inhibits
the formation of ice crystals, so this ice never freezes
really hard at domestic freezer temperatures and needs
no ripening before serving.*

—————— SERVES 6 ——————

2 juicy oranges
4 oz (120 g) caster sugar
4 fl oz (110 ml) water
1 pint (560 ml) non-vintage champagne
4 tablespoons brandy
¼ teaspoon angostura or orange bitters

Cut the peel from the oranges, using a very sharp knife,
taking only the zest and none of the pith. Squeeze,
strain and reserve the juice.

Put the orange zest, sugar and water into a saucepan
and heat gently until the sugar has dissolved completely. Raise the heat and boil the syrup for 5 minutes, then
set it aside to cool.

When the syrup is cold, discard the orange zest and
stir the orange juice, champagne, brandy and bitters
into the cold syrup.

Freeze in a sorbetière following the manufacturer's
instructions. Or still-freeze (page 4), vigorously whisking the partially frozen ice at least once during the
freezing process.

SORBET DE BEAUMES-DE-VENISE

*After years in the wilderness, dessert wines came back
into fashion with Muscat de Beaumes-de-Venise. With
its rich taste of muscat grapes, it is robust enough to
make an excellent ice with little in the way of other
additions. This is also true of many Barsacs, Tokays and
other sweet wines.*

—————— SERVES 6 ——————

4 oz (120 g) granulated or caster sugar
4 fl oz (110 ml) water
juice of 1 lemon
1 pint (560 ml) Muscat de Beaumes-de-Venise
1 egg white

Put the sugar and water into a small saucepan and heat
gently until the sugar has dissolved completely. Raise
the heat and boil the syrup for 5 minutes, then set it
aside to cool. Stir in the lemon juice and wine.

To freeze in a sorbetière: lightly whisk the egg white,
combine it with the syrup, then freeze immediately,
following the manufacturer's instructions.

To still-freeze (page 4): freeze the syrup to a heavy
slush, then whisk the egg whites until they are stiff and
beat them lightly into the partially frozen mixture.
Freeze until the ice is a little firmer, then vigorously
whisk once more for a really smooth sorbet. Return it to
the freezer until it is firm.

APPLE AND CALVADOS SORBET

Fresh fruit juice fortified with a liqueur of the same flavour makes a quick and elegant sorbet. Basic Sorbet Syrup speeds the process still further. Alternatively, make a syrup with 4 oz (120 g) granulated or caster sugar and 6 fl oz (170 ml) water. This ice will probably not require ripening, and can be served straight from the freezer.

——————— SERVES 6 ———————

¾ pint (420 ml) unsweetened apple juice
½ pint (280 ml) Basic Sorbet Syrup (page 78)
4 tablespoons fresh lemon juice
4 tablespoons calvados

Combine the apple juice with the sorbet syrup, lemon juice and calvados.

Freeze in a sorbetière following the manufacturer's instructions. Or still-freeze (page 4), vigorously whisking the partially frozen ice at least once during the freezing process.

PORT SLUSH

Port needs no additional sugar to make a superbly luxurious and alcoholic ice. This is a dense ice but does not freeze hard, so may be served straight from the freezer without ripening.

——————— SERVES 6 ———————

½ pint (280 ml) fresh orange juice
¾ pint (420 ml) port

Strain the orange juice and combine it with the port.

Freeze in a sorbetière following the manufacturer's instructions. Or still-freeze (page 4), vigorously whisking the partially frozen ice at least once during the freezing process.

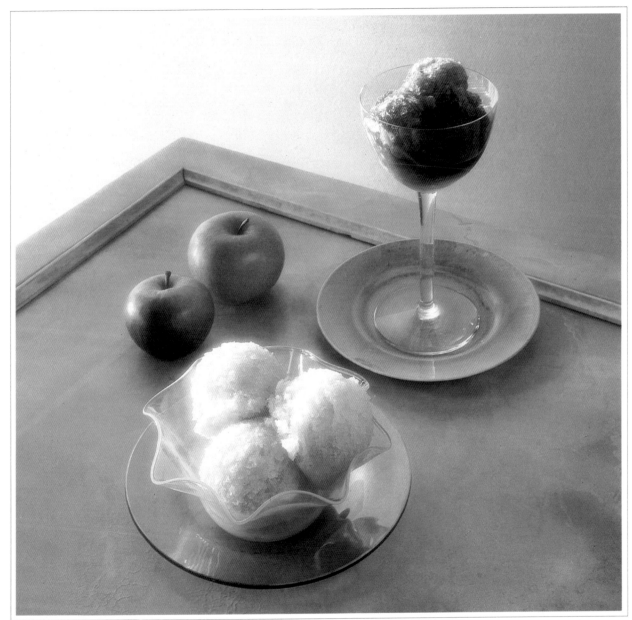

Left: Apple and Calvados Sorbet, right: Port Slush.

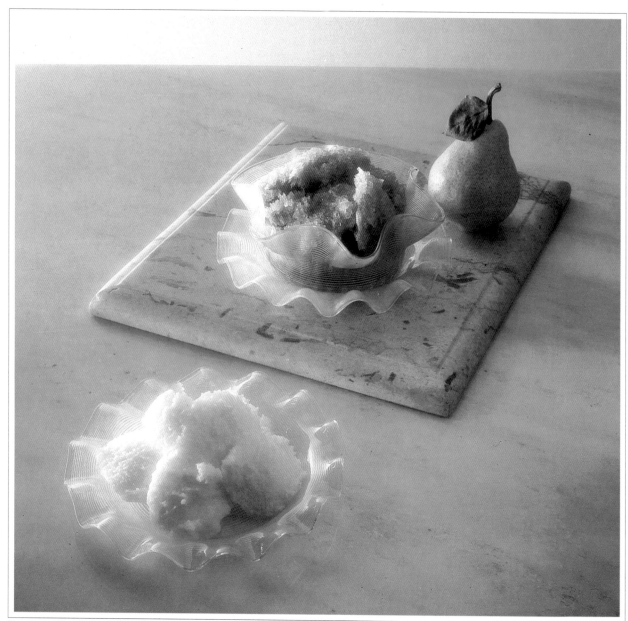

Top: Jaeger Tea Sorbet, below: Poire William Sorbet.

POIRE WILLIAM SORBET

All manner of fruits flavour the strong, colourless spirits which are especially popular in the mountainous regions of Europe. The pear and raspberry-flavoured varieties are the most successful in sorbets.

SERVES 6

8 oz (225 g) granulated sugar
12 fl oz (340 ml) water
6 tablespoons Poire William eau-de-vie
2 tablespoons fresh lemon juice
1 egg white

Put the sugar and water into a saucepan and heat gently until the sugar has dissolved completely. Raise the heat and boil the syrup for 5 minutes. Set it aside to cool. When the syrup is quite cold, stir in the Poire William eau-de-vie and lemon juice.

To freeze in a sorbetière: lightly whisk the egg white, combine it with the syrup, then freeze immediately, following the manufacturer's instructions.

To still-freeze (page 4): freeze the syrup to a heavy slush, then whisk the egg white until it is stiff and beat it lightly into the partially frozen mixture. Freeze until the ice is a little firmer, then vigorously whisk once more for a really smooth sorbet. Return it to the freezer.

JAEGER TEA SORBET

Jaeger tea – hot tea with rum – is Austria's version of the hot toddy. No doubt the Jaegers, or hunters, welcomed its cheer more warmly than a set of the good Dr Jaeger's long woolly underwear. To extract the maximum flavour and minimum tannin from any tea, use the following formula to calculate the optimum brewing time. Put the leaves into a heated container and pour freshly boiled water over them. The leaves will rise to the surface like the head on a pint of beer. Time how long they take to sink and you have that tea's ideal brewing time. Adjust the strength by altering the quantity of tea leaves. Indian or Ceylon tea is ideal for this sorbet.

SERVES 6

1 lemon
1½ pints (840 ml) strong black tea
4 oz (120 g) granulated, caster or soft light brown sugar
6 tablespoons rum

Cut the peel from the lemon, using a very sharp knife, taking only a thin layer of zest and none of the pith. Squeeze the juice and set it aside.

Put the tea into a saucepan with the sugar and lemon zest. Heat gently until the sugar has dissolved completely. Set it aside to cool completely, then discard the zest and stir in the rum.

Taste the syrup and add a little lemon juice to taste.

Freeze in a sorbetière following the manufacturer's instructions. Or still-freeze (page 4), vigorously whisking the partially frozen ice at least once during the freezing process.

VANILLA ICE CREAM

Real, old-fashioned vanilla ice cream made with an egg custard is the basis of many more perennial favourites. To transform it into cassata ice cream, stir a mixture of chopped dried and candied fruit into vanilla ice cream which has been frozen but is not yet quite firm. To make chocolate chip, grate hard chocolate, milk or plain, and stir it into the partially frozen ice. For rum and raisin, add raisins which have been soaked overnight in rum, or in a rum-flavoured syrup.

The recipe which follows is for a classic vanilla ice cream. Of course the quantity of sugar may be reduced by as much as half, and skimmed or semi-skimmed milk substituted for whole milk. The result will obviously be less rich and less sweet. It will also be a little crisper. Egg custards thicken below boiling point, and must not boil or they will curdle. It is a good idea to use a double boiler, or a bowl over simmering water.

———— SERVES 6 ————

1 vanilla pod or real vanilla extract
1¼ pints (700 ml) milk
6 egg yolks
10 oz (275 g) caster sugar
a pinch of salt

If using a vanilla pod, halve it lengthways and put it into a heavy saucepan with the milk. Heat gently to near boiling point, then remove from the heat and set it aside for 30 minutes. If using vanilla extract, there is no need to heat the milk. Add vanilla extract to taste once the custard has cooled.

Combine the egg yolks, sugar and salt in a bowl. Whisk until the mixture is very pale and falls back leaving a trail when the beaters are lifted. Strain the milk and gradually whisk it in. Return the mixture to the pan and cook it over a very low heat, or cook it in the top of a double boiler, stirring constantly until the custard is thick enough to coat the back of a wooden spoon.

Remove the custard from the heat and set it aside to cool, stirring it from time to time to prevent a skin forming. Vanilla extract should be added at this point, remembering that the flavour will fade with freezing.

Freeze in a sorbetière following the manufacturer's instructions. Or still-freeze (page 4), vigorously whisking the partially frozen ice at least once during the freezing process.

BUTTERSCOTCH ICE CREAM

Butter and soft brown sugar cooked together until the sugar caramelizes give a rich butterscotch flavour to this unusual ice.

———— SERVES 6 ————

3 oz (85 g) butter
8 oz (225 g) soft light brown sugar
1¼ pints (700 ml) hot milk
4 egg yolks, beaten

Melt the butter in a heavy saucepan and stir in the sugar. Cook the mixture slowly until the sugar begins to caramelize, watching it very carefully so that it does not become too dark. Remove from the heat and stir in the hot milk, and continue stirring until the toffee has dissolved completely.

Allow the flavoured milk to cool a little, then gradually stir it into the egg yolks in a bowl. Strain the mixture back into the pan and cook it carefully over a low heat, or cook it in the top of a double boiler, stirring constantly until the custard is thick enough to coat the back of a wooden spoon.

Remove the custard from the heat and set it aside to cool, stirring it from time to time to prevent a skin forming.

Freeze in a sorbetière following the manufacturer's instructions. Or still-freeze (page 4), vigorously whisking the partially frozen ice at least once during the freezing process.

Left: Chocolate Chip Ice Cream, centre: Butterscotch Ice Cream, right: Vanilla Ice Cream.

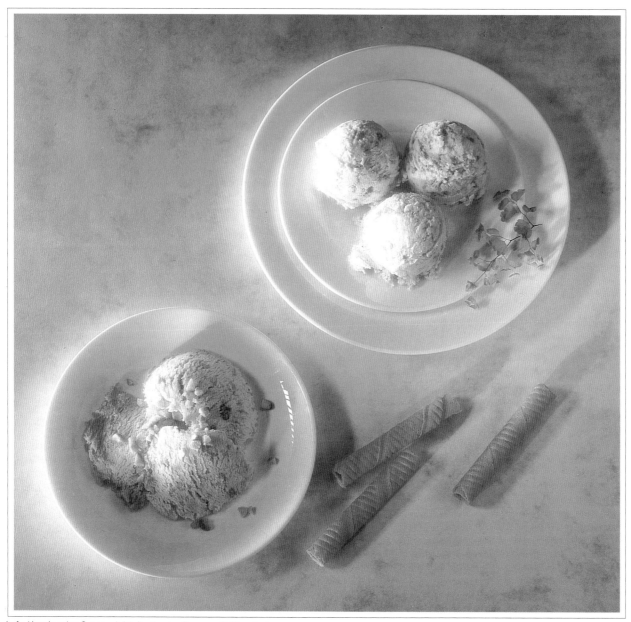

Left: Hazelnut Ice Cream, right: Praline Ice Cream with biscuit cigars.

PRALINE ICE CREAM

Toasted nuts and brittle caramel ground together to a fine powder are an indispensable flavouring in confectionery, pâtisserie and ices. Almonds and hazels are the best nuts for praline.

—————— SERVES 6 ——————

4 egg yolks
8 oz (225 g) caster sugar
¾ pint (420 ml) milk
2 oz (50 g) blanched almonds
¼ pint (150 ml) whipping cream

Heat the oven to 325°F (160°C, gas mark 3).

Combine the egg yolks with 6 oz (170 g) of the sugar in a bowl. Whisk until the mixture is very pale and falls back leaving a trail when the beaters are lifted. Gradually whisk in the milk.

Cook the custard carefully in a heavy saucepan over a low heat, or cook it in the top of a double boiler, stirring constantly until it is thick enough to coat the back of a wooden spoon. Take the custard off the heat and cool, stirring it from time to time to prevent a skin forming.

Meanwhile, spread the almonds on a baking sheet and toast them in the oven for about 10 minutes or until they are lightly browned. Then spread the almonds on a lightly oiled surface.

Put the remaining sugar and 4 tablespoons of water into a small, heavy saucepan and heat gently until it has dissolved and turns a deep golden brown. Immediately pour the caramel over the nuts – it does not matter if it does not cover all of them – and leave until cold. Then crush the praline to a fine powder in an electric coffee grinder or with a pestle and mortar.

Stir the praline into the cold custard. Whip the cream until it holds soft peaks and fold it in.

Freeze in a sorbetière following the manufacturer's instructions. Or still-freeze (page 4), vigorously whisking the partially frozen ice at least once during the freezing process.

HAZELNUT ICE CREAM

Nut ices are seldom available commercially and yet they are among the most appealing. Hazels, almonds, walnuts and pistachios all make excellent ice creams. Use the Vanilla Ice Cream custard base (page 24), omitting the vanilla flavouring, or try this richer recipe. Like hazelnuts, almonds are best toasted before grinding. Walnuts and pistachios need no cooking, but add a couple of tablespoons of sweet sherry to the walnut variation, and a few drops of almond essence to the custard for pistachio ice cream.

—————— SERVES 6 ——————

4 oz (120 g) shelled hazelnuts
4 egg yolks
6 oz (170 g) caster sugar
½ pint (280 ml) milk
½ pint (280 ml) whipping cream

Heat the oven to 325°F (160°C, gas mark 3).

Spread the hazelnuts on a baking sheet and toast them in the oven for 10-15 minutes, or until their centres are a pale biscuit colour. Turn the nuts on to a cloth and rub off the skins. Cool, then process them in a food processor or electric coffee mill. Set aside.

Combine the egg yolks and sugar in a bowl. Whisk until the mixture is very pale and falls back leaving a trail when the beaters are lifted. Gradually beat in the milk. Cook the custard carefully in a heavy saucepan over a low heat, or cook it in the top of a double boiler, stirring constantly until it is thick enough to coat the back of a wooden spoon. Take the custard off the heat and set it aside to cool, stirring it from time to time to prevent a skin forming.

Stir the ground hazelnuts into the cold custard. Whip the cream until it holds soft peaks and fold it in.

Freeze in a sorbetière following the manufacturer's instructions. Or still-freeze (page 4), vigorously whisking the partially frozen ice at least once during the freezing process.

CARDAMOM AND PISTACHIO ICE CREAM

The flavourings of this ice are Indian, but its creamy texture is decidedly European. Cardamom is an expensive spice, but only a little is needed in any one recipe. Scandinavians use it extensively in their baking and can buy ground cardamom with ease. When using the whole spice, remove the aromatic seeds from their surrounding pods and crush them with a little sugar with a pestle and mortar. For a real Indian touch, decorate each serving with edible silver leaf, found in Indian shops. This is real silver beaten out as thinly as tissue paper.

———— SERVES 6 ————

4 oz (120 g) granulated or caster sugar
4 fl oz (110 ml) water
¾ pint (420 ml) evaporated milk
about ¼ teaspoon ground cardamom
2 oz (50 g) shelled pistachio nuts, chopped
¼ pint (150 ml) whipping cream

Put the sugar and water into a heavy saucepan and heat gently until the sugar has dissolved completely. Raise the heat and boil the syrup for 5 minutes. Set it aside to cool, then stir in the evaporated milk, cardamom, pistachio nuts and lightly whipped cream.

Freeze in a sorbetière following the manufacturer's instructions. Or still-freeze (page 4), vigorously whisking the partially frozen ice at least once during the freezing process.

SAFFRON AND MACE ICE CREAM

A few strands of saffron are enough to perfume a whole batch of ice cream with the spice's earthy warmth and to colour it bright yellow. Mace, another warm spice, should be freshly ground if it is to be at its best. If mace is not available, use freshly grated nutmeg.

———— SERVES 6 ————

¼ teaspoon saffron strands
1¼ pints (700 ml) milk
6 egg yolks
10 oz (275 g) caster sugar
1 teaspoon ground mace

Put the saffron into a ladle and heat it over a naked flame to encourage it to release its colour and perfume. Take care that it does not darken too much or burn.

Put the milk and saffron into a large saucepan. Bring almost to the boil, then remove from the heat and leave to infuse for 30 minutes.

Combine the egg yolks and sugar in a bowl. Whisk until the mixture is very pale and falls back leaving a trail when the beaters are lifted. Strain the milk and gradually whisk it into the egg mixture.

Cook the custard carefully in a heavy saucepan over a low heat, or cook it in the top of a double boiler, stirring constantly until it is thick enough to coat the back of a wooden spoon. Remove the custard from the heat, stir in the mace and set it aside to cool, stirring it from time to time to prevent a skin forming.

Freeze in a sorbetière following the manufacturer's instructions. Or still-freeze (page 4), vigorously whisking the partially frozen ice at least once during the freezing process.

Left: Saffron and Mace Ice Cream, right: Cardamom and Pistachio Ice Cream with Tuiles (page 72).

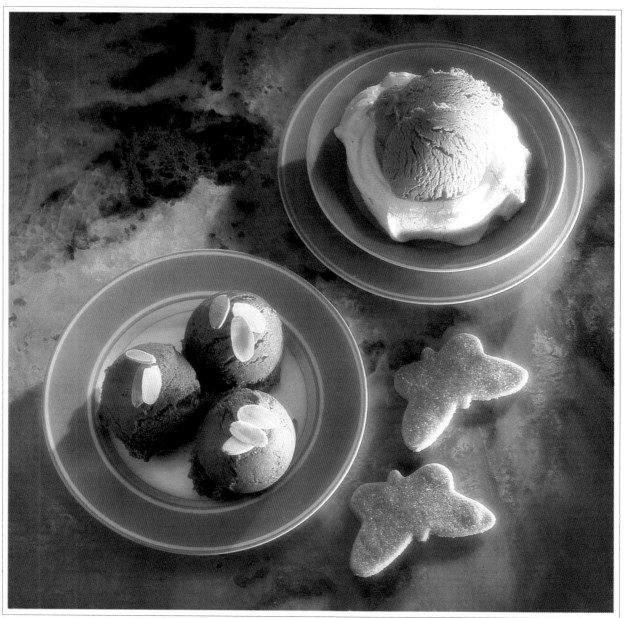

Left: Chocolate Ice Cream, centre: Butterfly Shortcake Thins (page 73), top: Coffee Ice Cream in Meringue Nest (page 76).

COFFEE ICE CREAM

Freshly roasted and ground coffee, especially if it is a high or dark roast, makes a superb flavouring for ices. Instant coffee can be used instead, of course, but the ice will have less distinction.

——————— SERVES 6 ———————

6 fl oz (170 ml) boiling water
4 tablespoons finely ground fresh coffee
6 egg yolks
8 oz (225 g) soft light brown sugar
1 pint (560 ml) milk

Use the water and coffee to make fresh filter coffee, or pour the water on to the coffee, infuse for a few minutes, then strain.

Combine the egg yolks and sugar in a bowl. Whisk until the mixture is very pale and falls back leaving a trail when the beaters are lifted. Whisk in the coffee and milk.

Cook the custard carefully in a heavy saucepan over a low heat, or cook it in the top of a double boiler, stirring constantly until it is thick enough to coat the back of a wooden spoon.

Take the custard off the heat, and set it aside to cool, stirring it from time to time to prevent a skin forming.

Freeze in a sorbetière following the manufacturer's instructions. Or still-freeze (page 4), vigorously whisking the partially frozen ice at least once during the freezing process.

CHOCOLATE ICE CREAM

This recipe uses good dark chocolate and avoids an over-sweet or over-rich mixture which would mask the chocolate flavour. Numerous variations on the basic formula are successful. To add a true orange flavour rub the skin of an orange with a half dozen sugar cubes and dissolve them in the hot custard. Or combine the partially frozen ice with flaked almonds which have been toasted lightly and cooled.

——————— SERVES 6 ———————

6 egg yolks
4 oz (120 g) caster sugar
½ pint (280 ml) milk
½ pint (280 ml) single cream
8 oz (225 g) good-quality dark chocolate, grated
real vanilla extract

Combine the egg yolks and sugar in a bowl. Whisk until the mixture is very pale and falls back in a trail when the beaters are lifted. Whisk in the milk, followed by the cream.

Cook the custard carefully in a heavy saucepan over a low heat, or cook it in the top of a double boiler, stirring constantly until it is thick enough to coat the back of a wooden spoon. Remove it from the heat.

Stir the chocolate into the hot custard, then add a few drops of vanilla extract. Leave the custard to cool, stirring it from time to time to prevent a skin forming.

Freeze in a sorbetière following the manufacturer's instructions. Or still-freeze (page 4), vigorously whisking the partially frozen ice at least once during the freezing process.

LECHE MERENGADA

Spanish cinnamon ices are classics of another kind – crisp milk ices lightened with egg whites. This recipe is adapted from one given in The Foods and Wines of Spain *by Penelope Casas (Penguin Books, 1985).*

─────────── SERVES 6 ───────────

1 lemon
1 pint (560 ml) milk
8 fl oz (225 ml) double cream
6 oz (170 g) caster sugar
2 × 4-in (10-cm) cinnamon sticks
2 egg whites
ground cinnamon

Cut the peel from the lemon, using a very sharp knife, taking only the zest and none of the pith. Squeeze the lemon and reserve the juice.

Put the lemon zest into a heavy saucepan with the milk, cream, sugar and cinnamon sticks and heat gently, stirring until the sugar has dissolved completely. Then raise the heat and simmer the mixture for about 30 minutes. Set it aside to cool completely, then discard the lemon zest and cinnamon sticks.

Whisk the egg whites with a teaspoon of the lemon juice until they hold soft peaks. Beat in the flavoured milk.

Freeze in a sorbetière following the manufacturer's instructions. Or still-freeze (page 4), vigorously whisking the partially frozen ice at least once during the freezing process. Dust each serving with a little ground cinnamon.

BROWN BREAD ICE CREAM

Ices made with toasted brown breadcrumbs have been popular in England since the latter half of the eighteenth century. The Victorians decorated this ice with crystallized violets (page 78). Fresh raspberries are good too. Use robust wholemeal bread for this recipe.

─────────── SERVES 6 ───────────

3 oz (85 g) wholemeal breadcrumbs
3 oz (85 g) granulated sugar
4 tablespoons water
¾ pint (420 ml) double cream
2 oz (50 g) icing sugar, sifted
2 tablespoons rum
real vanilla extract

Spread the crumbs on a baking tray and toast under a grill, stirring from time to time, until an even golden brown. Be careful not to burn them. Set aside to cool.

Put the sugar and water into a saucepan and heat gently until the sugar has dissolved completely. Wash down any crystals from the sides of the pan with a pastry brush dipped in cold water. Raise the heat and boil the syrup to a rich brown caramel. Do not allow the caramel to darken too much or it will be bitter. Take it off the heat and stir in the crumbs.

Immediately turn the mixture on to a buttered baking tray. It will harden quickly to a kind of poor man's praline. Grind it finely in a coffee grinder or with a pestle and mortar. Do not try to grind this very hard mixture in a food processor or blender. It may damage the blades. Whip the cream until it holds soft peaks, then beat in the icing sugar, rum and a little vanilla extract. Fold in the sugared crumbs and still-freeze (page 4) without stirring.

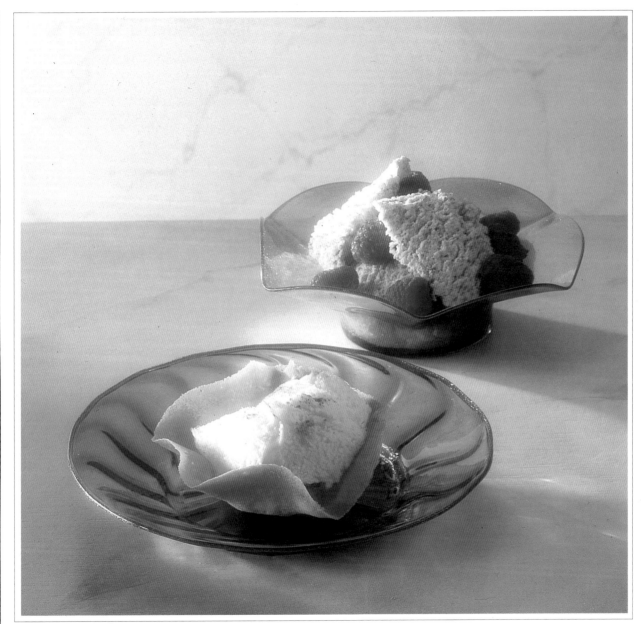

Top: Brown Bread Ice Cream, below: Leche Merengada in Tuile Basket (page 72).

Left: Honey Ice Cream with Lavender (page 36), centre: Rich Vanilla
Ice Cream (page 36) in Brandy Snap Basket (page 73), right:
Lemon Ice Cream.

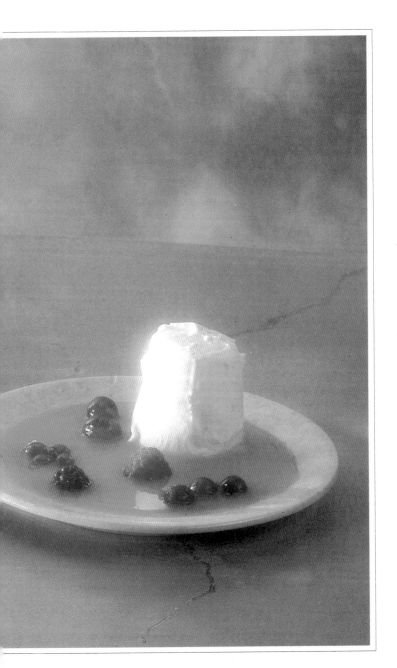

LEMON ICE CREAM

Smooth, creamy ices that can be frozen without stirring are quick and easy to make, but they do tend to be rich. It is the quantity of cream that makes these mixtures freeze successfully without requiring constant beating to reduce the size of the ice crystals.
This lemon ice cream is quite simply sumptuous, as are Seville orange or lime ice creams made in the same manner. It may be frozen in individual serving containers – hollowed out lemons are most attractive. It can also be used as a piped topping for more elaborate frozen desserts.

SERVES 6

3 juicy lemons
6 oz (170 g) icing sugar
¾ pint (420 ml) double cream
3 tablespoons iced water

Using the finest blade on the grater, grate the zest from 2 of the lemons, and squeeze the juice from all 3. Combine the zest, juice and sugar and if possible set aside for 30 minutes to allow the flavour to develop.

Whip the cream with the water until it holds soft peaks, then whisk in the sweetened lemon juice. Turn the mixture into a shallow freezer tray, individual serving dishes or hollowed out lemons. Cover and still-freeze (page 4), without stirring, until firm.

RICH VANILLA ICE CREAM
Illustrated on pages 34/35

Condensed milk provides the sweetening in this very easily-made ice.

———————— SERVES 6 ————————

½ pint (280 ml) double cream, well chilled
6 fl oz (170 g) tinned condensed milk, well chilled
real vanilla extract

Put the cream and condensed milk into a bowl, add vanilla extract to taste, and whip until the mixture holds soft peaks. When adding the flavouring, remember that freezing will dull its intensity.

Turn the mixture into a shallow freezer tray, or into individual serving dishes. Cover and still-freeze (page 4), without stirring, until firm.

HONEY ICE CREAM WITH LAVENDER
Illustrated on pages 34/35

Lavender flowers are commonly used as a herb in the south of France, and pungent lavender-perfumed honey is sold from roadside stalls at the edges of purple cushioned fields.

———————— SERVES 6 ————————

6 oz (170 g) lavender honey
¾ pint (420 ml) whipping cream
1 teaspoon fresh lavender flowers

If the honey is thick, thin it down with a little of the cream. Whip the remaining cream until it holds soft peaks and fold in the honey and lavender flowers.

Turn the mixture into a shallow freezer tray or individual serving dishes. Cover and still-freeze (page 4) without stirring until firm.

BANANA ICE CREAM

Illustrated on page 39

A little of this rich banana ice cream goes a long way.

──────── SERVES 6 ────────

1 lb (450 g) ripe bananas
4 oz (120 g) icing sugar
juice of 1 orange, or 3 tablespoons rum
½ pint (280 ml) double cream

Mash or process the peeled bananas with the icing sugar and orange juice or rum. Whip the cream until it holds soft peaks. Fold the banana purée into the cream.

Turn the mixture into a shallow freezer tray or individual serving dishes. Cover and still-freeze (page 4), without stirring, until firm.

RATAFIA ICE CREAM

Illustrated on page 39

Ratafia Biscuits are an excellent use for spare egg whites. They are easy to make (page 74) and excellent in ice cream as well as with it. This ice cream goes particularly well with a fruit sauce, such as raspberry or peach.

──────── SERVES 6 ────────

4 oz (120 g) Ratafia Biscuits (page 74)
¾ pint (420 ml) whipping cream
4 oz (120 g) icing sugar
almond or ratafia essence to taste

Crush the ratafias to coarse crumbs. Whip the cream with the icing sugar and a little almond or ratafia essence until it holds soft peaks. Fold in the crushed ratafias.

Turn the mixture into a shallow freezer tray or individual serving dishes. Cover and still-freeze (page 4), without stirring, until firm.

CHESTNUT ICE CREAM

A tin of chestnut purée, sweetened and lightly flavoured with vanilla, is a useful standby in any store-cupboard. As a variation on this easy ice cream recipe, stir a handful of broken meringue into the ice when it is partially frozen, then freeze until firm. It can be served sprinkled with flaked chocolate.

————————— SERVES 6 —————————

8 oz (225 g) tinned sweetened chestnut purée
2 tablespoons sweet sherry or milk
½ pint (280 ml) whipping cream
2 oz (50 g) icing sugar

Combine the chestnut purée with the sherry or milk, and mix to a smooth paste.

Whip the cream with the icing sugar until it holds soft peaks, and fold it into the chestnut purée.

Turn the mixture into a shallow freezer tray or individual serving dishes. Cover and still-freeze (page 4), without stirring, until firm.

CHAZEL ICE CREAM

Chocolate and hazelnuts taste marvellous together — as confectioners have long appreciated — in this really speedy ice cream.

————————— SERVES 6 —————————

¾ pint (420 ml) whipping cream
4 oz (120 g) chocolate and hazelnut spread
2 oz (50 g) icing sugar

Stir about 6 tablespoons of the cream into the chocolate and hazelnut spread. Whip the remaining cream with the icing sugar until it holds soft peaks. Fold the chocolate and hazelnut mixture into the cream.

Turn the mixture into a shallow freezer tray or individual serving dishes. Cover and still-freeze (page 4), without stirring, until firm.

Above: Chazel Ice Cream with Tear-drop Shortcake Thins (page 73).

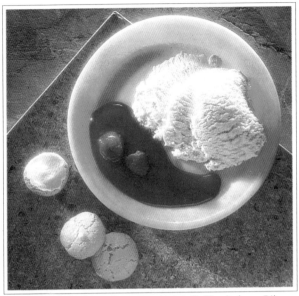

Above: Ratafia Ice Cream (page 37) with Ratafia Biscuits (page 74).

Above: Banana Ice Cream (page 37).

Above: Chestnut Ice Cream.

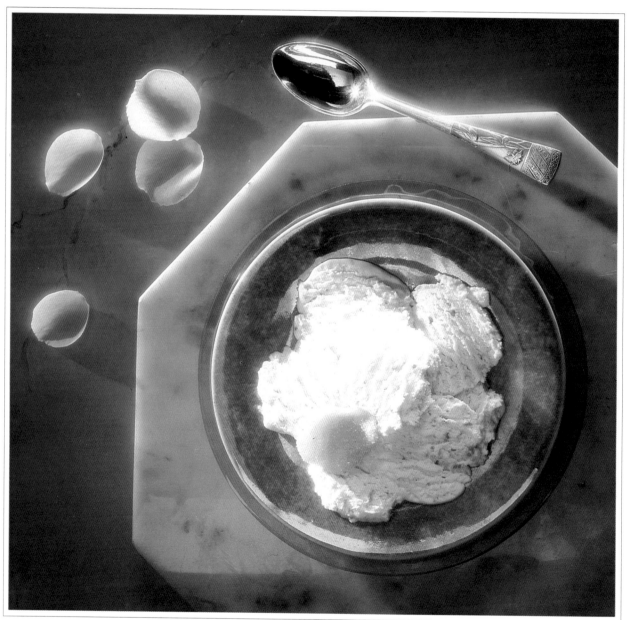

Above: Rose Petal Ice Cream.

ROSE PETAL ICE CREAM

Candied rose petals and rosewater perfume this romantic sounding ice. The strength of rosewater varies, so add a teaspoonful at a time and taste. It will look the part too if decorated with whole crystallized rose petals (page 78).

—————— SERVES 6 ——————

2 oz (50 g) candied rose petals
4 oz (120 g) icing sugar
¾ pint (420 ml) double cream
rosewater to taste

Crush the candied rose petals almost to a powder. Combine the icing sugar with the cream and whisk until the mixture holds soft peaks. Fold in the candied rose petals and add rosewater a little at a time, bearing in mind that freezing will dull the flavouring.

Turn the mixture into a shallow freezer tray or individual serving dishes, and still-freeze (page 4), without stirring, until firm.

STRAWBERRY ICE CREAM

Illustration on page 43

Ripe fruit that is full of flavour is the essential ingredient of strawberry ice cream, and as long as damaged parts of the berries are discarded, there is no better use for less than perfect specimens. The orange and lemon juice helps to bring out the flavour of the strawberries. The same technique and recipe is also suitable for raspberries.

—————— SERVES 6 ——————

12 oz (340 g) ripe strawberries, hulled
juice of 1 orange
juice of 1 lemon
6 oz (170 g) caster sugar
¾ pint (420 ml) whipping cream

Rub the berries through a sieve, or process them briefly in a blender or food processor and strain the purée.

Combine the purée with the orange and lemon juice and sugar. Set the mixture aside for about 2 hours, stirring it from time to time until the sugar has dissolved completely. (This step intensifies the flavour of the fruit.)

Whip the cream until it holds soft peaks, combine it with the sweetened purée and whisk them lightly together.

Freeze in a sorbetière following the manufacturer's instructions. Or still-freeze (page 4), vigorously whisking the partially frozen ice at least once during the freezing process.

DAMSON ICE CREAM

For flavour, damsons and greengages are the aristocrats of the plum family, and both make excellent ices. Damson ice cream is smooth, rich and assertively flavoured.

—————— SERVES 6 ——————

1 lb (450 g) damsons
4 oz (120 g) soft light brown sugar
½ pint (280 ml) water
4 egg yolks
4 oz (120 g) icing sugar
½ pint (280 ml) double cream
2 tablespoons iced water

Put the damsons into a saucepan with the brown sugar and ½ pint (280 ml) water and bring to the boil. Cover and simmer the fruit until it is tender, about 10 minutes depending on the ripeness of the damsons.

Press the stewed fruit through a sieve. Discard the stones and chill the purée in the refrigerator.

In a bowl set over a saucepan of simmering water, beat the egg yolks with the icing sugar until the mixture is warm but not hot. Take the bowl off the heat and continue beating until the mixture has tripled its original volume, then chill it in the refrigerator.

Whisk the cream with the iced water until it holds soft peaks. Combine the damson purée, egg mixture and whipped cream and whisk them lightly together.

Freeze in a sorbetière following the manufacturer's instructions. Or still-freeze (page 4), vigorously whisking the partially frozen ice at least once during the freezing process.

PRUNE ICE CREAM

Liberate the humble prune from its custard and sniggers schoolboy image by transforming it into this rich, grown-up ice. Prune ice cream is a worthy candidate for a slosh of optional alcohol. Almost any spirit, from gin to cognac, does the trick. Use Indian or China tea at normal strength for this recipe. You can use the same recipe to make a golden ice cream with dried apricots.

—————— SERVES 6 ——————

1 lb (450 g) plump prunes
about 1½ pints (840 ml) cold tea
zest of half an orange
4 oz (120 g) soft light brown sugar
½ pint (280 ml) whipping cream
2 tablespoons gin (optional)

Put the prunes into a bowl with the orange zest and add enough cold tea to cover them. Leave them to soak for several hours, preferably overnight, then add the sugar and simmer in a saucepan until tender. Set them aside until they are cool enough to handle.

Stone the prunes and discard the orange zest. Purée the fruit with the cooking syrup either by passing it through a sieve, or processing it in a blender or food processor and then straining it. Stir in the gin, if used.

Whisk the cream until it holds soft peaks then combine it with the prune purée.

Freeze in a sorbetière following the manufacturer's instructions. Or still-freeze (page 4), vigorously whisking the partially frozen ice at least once during the freezing process.

Top: Damson Ice Cream with langue du chat biscuits, centre: Prune Ice Cream, below: Strawberry Ice Cream (page 41).

Above: Coconut Ice Cream

Above: Melon and Ginger Ice Cream.

Above: Mango Ice Cream.

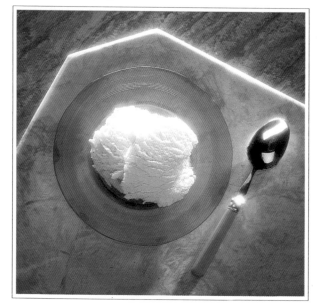

Above: Nectarine Ice Cream.

MELON AND GINGER ICE CREAM

A really ripe melon, one that is so heavily perfumed that its character is plain, will make a memorable ice cream.

———— SERVES 6 ————

1 ripe melon about 1 lb (450 g)
juice of 1 lemon
6 oz (170 g) soft light brown sugar
10 fl oz (280 ml) whipping cream
2 oz (50 g) crystallized ginger, finely chopped

Halve the melon, discard the seeds and spoon out the flesh. Purée it by pressing it through a sieve, or by processing it in a blender or food processor and straining it. Add the lemon juice and sugar to the purée and leave the mixture to stand for about 2 hours, stirring it from time to time until the sugar has dissolved.

Whisk the cream until it holds soft peaks, then combine it with the melon purée and the ginger. Freeze in a sorbetière following the manufacturer's instructions. Or still-freeze (page 4), vigorously whisking the partially frozen ice at least once during freezing.

MANGO ICE CREAM

Fully ripe mangoes are heavily perfumed, sumptuously flavoured and quickly made into a rich ice cream. Perfectly ripe peaches and nectarines can also be used.

———— SERVES 6 ————

2 large ripe mangoes
juice of 1 lime or lemon
2 oz (50 g) icing sugar
½ pint (280 ml) whipping cream

Peel the mangoes and cut the flesh from the stones. Purée the flesh with the lime or lemon juice either by processing it lightly in a blender or food processor, or by passing it through a sieve. Stir in the icing sugar.

Whip the cream until it holds soft peaks. Whisk the purée lightly into the cream.

Freeze in a sorbetière following the manufacturer's instructions. Or still-freeze (page 4), vigorously whisking the partially frozen ice at least once during the freezing process.

COCONUT ICE CREAM

Fresh coconut ices are made throughout the tropics. Desiccated coconut, too, gives excellent results.

———— SERVES 6 ————

1½ pints (840 ml) milk
8 oz (225 g) desiccated coconut
6 egg yolks
6 oz (170 g) caster sugar

Bring the milk to the boil in a saucepan and stir in the desiccated coconut. Set the mixture aside to infuse for at least 1 hour, then strain it through a fine sieve, pressing the coconut to extract most of the flavour.

Combine the egg yolks and sugar in a bowl. Whisk until the mixture is very pale and leaves a trail when the beaters are lifted. Gradually whisk in the coconut--flavoured milk.

Return the mixture to the pan and cook it over a very low heat, or cook it in the top of a double boiler, stirring constantly until the custard is thick enough to coat the back of a wooden spoon.

Remove the custard from the heat to cool, stirring it from time to time to prevent a skin forming.

Freeze in a sorbetière following the manufacturer's instructions. Or still-freeze (page 4), vigorously whisking the partially frozen ice at least once during the freezing process.

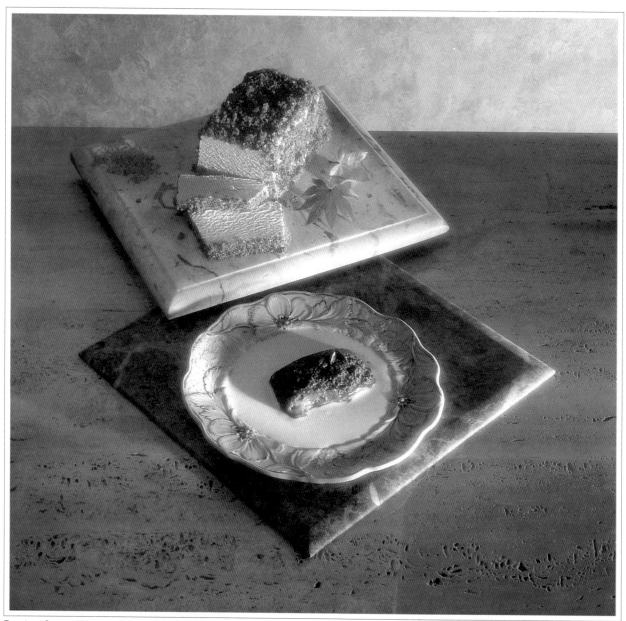

Top: Iced Caramel Mousse, below: Chocolate Marquise.

ICED CARAMEL MOUSSE

Use Ratafias (page 74), amaretti biscuits, or chocolate digestives for the crumb covering of this mousse.

———— SERVES 6 ————

8 oz (225 g) sugar
juice of 1 lemon
1 tablespoon powdered gelatine
2 egg whites
a pinch of salt
½ pint (280 ml) double cream
4 oz (120 g) biscuit crumbs

Prepare a 2-lb (900-g) loaf tin by lining it with baking parchment or foil.

Put the sugar and 6 tablespoons of water in a heavy saucepan and heat gently, stirring, until the sugar has dissolved completely. Wash down any crystals from the sides of the pan with a pastry brush dipped in cold water. Raise the heat and cook the sugar until it turns a rich golden brown. Watch it carefully because if it darkens too much the caramel will be bitter.

As soon as the caramel is sufficiently coloured, take the pan off the heat and immediately dip its base in cold water to stop the temperature rising further. Stir in ¼ pint (150 ml) water. The caramel will set hard on contact with the water, but will soon melt again with an occasional stir. Cool completely to a brown syrup.

Put the lemon juice into a small saucepan with 2 tablespoons of water and sprinkle the gelatine over it. Set it aside for a few minutes to let it swell and soften. Then heat very gently, without allowing it to boil, until the gelatine is completely melted. Stir the warm liquid gelatine into the caramel syrup and set it aside until it is cool and beginning to set.

Whisk the egg whites with a pinch of salt until they hold firm peaks. Whip the cream until it too holds firm peaks. Combine the caramel syrup with the whisked egg whites and cream and whisk them together lightly. Turn the mixture into the prepared loaf tin and freeze.

Remove the frozen mousse from the tin and strip off its lining papers. Allow the outside to soften a little, then press the biscuit crumbs all over the surface. Return the dessert to the freezer until it is needed. If it is to be stored for more than an hour or two it should be covered to prevent ice crystals forming on it.

CHOCOLATE MARQUISE

Very rich and dark, a Chocolate Marquise is frozen in a brick-shaped loaf tin and sliced, straight from the freezer. Serve a slice on a plate which has been flooded with a layer of vanilla or coffee sauce – simply the custard bases of those ices, before freezing. Variations to a basic marquise can include broken meringue or rum-soaked raisins.

———— SERVES 6 ————

8 oz (225 g) dark chocolate
4 oz (120 g) unsalted butter, diced
2 large eggs, separated
a pinch of salt
3 oz (85 g) icing sugar
for the decoration
dark-roast coffee beans

Grate or break the chocolate into a bowl and add the butter. Heat gently over a pan of simmering water, stirring until the mixture is smooth.

In a second bowl whisk the egg whites with the salt until they hold stiff peaks. In a third bowl beat the egg yolks with the sugar until the mix is pale and fluffy.

Mix the melted chocolate lightly into the yolk mixture, then fold in the whisked whites. Spoon the mixture into a non-stick 2-lb (900-g) loaf tin, cover the top with foil and freeze until firm.

To serve, turn the marquise on to a chilled serving plate. Decorate the top with a few glossy coffee beans.

Left: Passion Fruit Parfait, right: Liqueur Parfaits.

LIQUEUR PARFAITS

Parfaits are rich, smooth ices. They are often flavoured with liqueurs and frozen in individual serving dishes. Stemmed coloured glasses also make pretty containers. Or the rims of plain glasses can be frosted with plain or coloured sugar. For orange sugar frosting to go with a Cointreau or Grand Marnier parfait, dip the rims of the glasses first in undiluted orange squash then immediately into granulated sugar. Chill them until needed. If you are using tall glasses, check that they have room to stand in the freezer.

—————— SERVES 6 ——————

8 oz (225 g) granulated sugar
6 tablespoons water
4 egg yolks
4 tablespoons liqueur
2 egg whites
8 fl oz (225 ml) whipping cream

Put the sugar into a small, heavy saucepan with the water and heat gently, stirring, until the sugar has dissolved completely. Wash down any sugar crystals from the sides of the pan with a pastry brush dipped in cold water, then raise the heat and boil the syrup until it is just beginning to colour (about 310°F/154°C on a sugar thermometer).

Take the pan off the heat and set it aside to cool for 1 minute. In the meantime, put the egg yolks into a large bowl and whisk them to a froth. Gradually whisk in the hot syrup, and when it has been added, continue whisking until the mixture is cool and has tripled its original volume. Whisk in the liqueur, then chill the mixture in the refrigerator.

Whisk the egg whites until they hold stiff peaks. Whip the cream until it holds soft peaks. Combine the yolk mixture with the whisked egg whites and cream and whisk them together lightly. Turn the parfait into individual dishes and freeze until firm.

PASSION FRUIT PARFAIT

Passion fruit has a strong flavour and perfume which can stand dilution with eggs and cream. The ripe fruit look most unpromising, but until the skins are withered their perfume will be less than its best. To extract the flesh, open passion fruit like soft boiled eggs and spoon out the seedy interiors. Freeze the parfait in individual glasses, or in a decorative ice cream mould.

—————— SERVES 6 ——————

4 ripe passion fruit
8 oz (225 g) granulated sugar
6 tablespoons water
4 egg yolks
2 egg whites
8 fl oz (225 ml) whipping cream

Sieve the passion fruit pulp to extract the seeds. The amount of juice left to flavour the parfait will be small, but powerful.

Put the sugar and water into a small, heavy saucepan and heat gently, stirring, until the sugar has dissolved completely. Wash down any crystals from the sides of the pan with a pastry brush dipped in cold water. Raise the heat and boil the syrup until it is just beginning to colour (about 310°F/154°C on a sugar thermometer).

Take the pan off the heat and set it aside to cool for 1 minute. While it is cooling, put the egg yolks into a large bowl and whisk them to a froth. Gradually whisk in the hot syrup, and when it has all been added, continue whisking until the mixture is cool and has tripled its original volume. Whisk in the strained passion fruit juice, then chill the mixture in the refrigerator.

Whisk the egg whites until they hold stiff peaks. Whip the cream until it holds soft peaks. Then combine the yolk mixture with the whisked egg whites and cream and whisk them together lightly.

Turn the parfait into individual dishes or into a mould and freeze until firm. Serve on its own or with a fresh Fruit Coulis (page 77), such as a mango purée.

49

ICED RASPBERRY SOUFFLE

Iced soufflés are every bit as dramatic as the hot kind and involve no strain on the cook's nervous system. An iced soufflé cannot flop. Raspberries are ideal for this type of soufflé because their flavour survives dispersal through a cloud of whipped cream and meringue.

SERVES 6

12 oz (340 g) ripe raspberries, fresh or frozen and thawed
4 oz (120 g) caster sugar
2 tablespoons orange liqueur, or fresh orange juice
2 egg whites
2 oz (50 g) icing sugar
¾ pint (420 ml) whipping cream

Wrap a strip of double thickness baking parchment or oiled greaseproof paper round the outside of a straight-sided 1¾-pint (1-litre) soufflé dish, or round 6 individual ramekins. The paper should come 2 ins (5 cms) above the rim of the dish, or dishes, to make a collar. Secure the join with a pin, and chill the dish, or dishes.

Set aside a dozen perfect raspberries to decorate the finished soufflé. Purée the remaining raspberries either by pressing the fruit through a fine sieve to remove the pips, or by processing them briefly in a blender or food processor and straining the pulp. Stir in the caster sugar and orange liqueur (or juice). Set aside for at least 1 hour to allow the flavour to develop, stirring from time to time until the sugar has dissolved.

Whisk the egg whites until they hold soft peaks then add the icing sugar and whisk until the mixture holds firm peaks. Whip the cream until it holds soft peaks.

Whisk the purée, whisked egg whites and cream together lightly and immediately turn the mixture into the prepared dish or dishes. Smooth the top and cover with foil — keeping it away from the top of the soufflé — and freeze until firm.

Remove the foil and the paper collar before ripening the soufflé to serve it. Decorate the top with the reserved raspberries.

ICED PEAR SOUFFLE

Illustrated on page 52

Poire William eau-de-vie underlines the pear flavour in this lovely, light, iced soufflé. Use the same recipe to make other flavours with fresh fruits and their own fruit-flavoured liqueurs. Or use a little kirsch instead.

SERVES 6

1 lb (450 g) dessert or cooking pears, peeled and cored
juice of 1 lemon
½ pint (280 ml) double cream
4 tablespoons Poire William eau-de-vie or kirsch
1 cooked Meringue (page 76)

Wrap a strip of double thickness baking parchment or oiled greaseproof paper round the outside of a straight-sided 1¾-pint (1-litre) soufflé dish, or round 6 individual ramekins. The paper should come 2 ins (5 cms) above the rim of the dish, or dishes, to make a collar. Secure the join with a pin, and chill the dish, or dishes, until they are needed.

Chop the pears roughly and turn the pieces in the lemon juice to prevent them from discolouring. Cook them until tender in a stainless steel or enamelled saucepan with a little water, if needed. Or bake the pears, covered, in a moderate oven (350°F/180°C, gas mark 4). Timing will depend on the ripeness of the pears.

Cool the cooked pears and purée them either by passing them through a sieve, or by processing them in a blender or food processor. Set the purée aside to cool.

Whip the cream with the eau-de-vie (or kirsch) until it holds soft peaks. Combine the pear purée with the meringue and whipped cream and whisk them together lightly. Turn the mixture into the prepared dish, or dishes and cover with foil. Freeze until firm.

Remove the foil lid and the paper collar before ripening the soufflé to serve it. Spoonfuls of the soufflé may also be served in Tuile or Brandy Snap Baskets (page 72/73).

Above: Iced Raspberry Soufflé.

Top: Zabaglione Semi Freddo, centre: Iced Pear Soufflé (page 50), below: Iced Maple Pecan Soufflé in Tuile Basket (page 72).

ZABAGLIONE SEMI FREDDO

Zabaglione is the simplest of spectacular puddings – just egg yolks, sugar and marsala, for which a medium or sweet sherry may be substituted at a pinch. In its warm form, zabaglione has to be made just before it is served. But this iced version is a more practical proposition for entertaining.

--------- SERVES 6 ---------

4 egg yolks
4 oz (120 g) caster sugar
¼ pint (150 ml) dry marsala
¼ pint (150 ml) whipping cream

Put the egg yolks into a fairly large bowl (ideally made of copper) which will fit over a pan. Add the sugar and whisk until the mixture is very pale and falls back leaving a trail when the beaters are lifted.

Whisk in the marsala, then set the bowl over a pan of simmering water and continue whisking until the mixture has at least doubled its volume. Take off the heat and set the bowl in cold water, or over ice, and whisk until the mixture is cool.

Whip the cream until it holds soft peaks. Combine it with the cold zabaglione and whisk them together lightly.

Turn the mixture into small stemmed glasses or individual dishes and freeze until firm. Serve with crisp, buttery Classic Tuiles (page 72).

ICED MAPLE PECAN SOUFFLE

Real maple syrup tastes so much better than the cheaper synthetic kind that it is worth searching out. It keeps almost indefinitely which is more than can be said of pecans or any other nuts for that matter. The oil in old or badly stored nuts gradually turns rancid, so it is a good idea to taste shelled nuts before using them in a recipe.

--------- SERVES 6 ---------

1 tablespoon powdered gelatine
4 tablespoons water
4 fl oz (110 ml) maple syrup
3 eggs, separated
a pinch of salt
2 oz (50 g) icing sugar
¾ pint (420 ml) double cream
2 oz (50 g) shelled pecans, chopped
for the decoration
pecan halves

Wrap a strip of double thickness baking parchment or oiled greaseproof paper round the outside of a straight-sided 1¾-pint (1-litre) soufflé dish, or round 6 individual ramekins. The paper should come 2 ins (5 cms) above the rim of the dish, or dishes, to make a collar. Secure the join with a pin, and chill the dish, or dishes.

Sprinkle the gelatine over the water in a small pan and set it aside for a few minutes until the gelatine has softened and swollen. Heat very gently, stirring, without allowing it to boil, until the gelatine has melted completely. Set aside.

Put the maple syrup and egg yolks into a bowl over a pan of simmering water and whisk until the mixture is lukewarm. Take the bowl off the heat and continue whisking until the mixture is cool and has tripled its original volume.

In a second bowl whisk the egg whites with a pinch of salt, until they are foamy, then add the icing sugar and whisk until the mixture holds stiff peaks. >

<In a third bowl whip the cream until it holds soft peaks.

Combine the gelatine with the yolk mixture, whisked egg whites and whipped cream and whisk them together lightly. Fold in the chopped pecans and turn the mixture into the prepared dish or dishes. Cover with a lid of foil – keeping it away from the top of the soufflé – and freeze until firm.

Remove the foil and the paper collar before ripening the soufflé to serve it. Top with the pecan halves.

If there is time for last-minute messing about, dip the decorative nuts in liquid caramel (4 oz (120 g) sugar cooked with 4 tablespoons water until golden brown) and set them on a greased surface to cool and harden.

KNICKERBOCKER GLORY

King of coupes is the one and only Knickerbocker Glory. It has an extravagance that appeals to the child in the staidest adult and one of the few places still serving the genuine article is the Soda Fountain at Fortnum and Mason in London's Piccadilly.
The glass for a Knickerbocker Glory should be tall and fluted like a giant ice cream cone. It is then filled to brimming with ices, fruit and cream.

─────────── FOR 1 SERVING ───────────

sugared raspberries
crushed pineapple
1 scoop Vanilla Ice Cream (page 24)
1 scoop Strawberry Ice Cream (page 41)
1 tablespoon whipped cream, or to taste
a maraschino or glacé cherry

Put a little of the fruit in the bottom of the glass and top with the ices and remaining fruit in any order. Pipe a generous dollop of whipped cream on top and crown with the cherry.

Left: Knickerbocker Glory, centre: Nutcase (page 56), right: Big
Business (page 56), with a florentine wafer and pompadour fan wafers.

COUPES – SIX OF THE BEST

Coupes do not have to be fancy or festooned with cream to succeed. One of the best is the simplest I know. In France the classic combination of lemon sorbet and iced vodka is called 'le colonel' and it is as subtle and sophisticated an ice as you will meet.

Coupe Cassis: another perennially popular combination of ices and fruit, in this case blackcurrants. In a glass or dish combine a scoop of Vanilla Ice Cream (page 24) with a scoop of Blackcurrant Sorbet (page 16) and fresh or lightly stewed blackcurrants. Add a tablespoon of blackcurrant alcohol (crème de cassis) or syrup, and top with Chantilly Cream (page 76).

Big Business: a scoop of Chocolate Ice Cream (page 31), another of Chocolate Chip Ice Cream (page 24) and a spoonful each of Hot Chocolate Sauce and Chocolate Fudge Sauce (page 77).

English Garden: a scoop of Apple and Honey Sorbet (page 6), another of Apple and Calvados Sorbet (page 20) served with Raspberry Coulis (page 77) and topped with red berries, whichever are in season.

Tippler: Rum and Raisin Ice Cream (page 24) with broken Ratafia Biscuits (page 74), Raspberry Coulis (page 77), Jaeger Tea Sorbet (page 23) and a Chantilly Cream Topping (page 76).

Nutcase: scoops of Praline Ice Cream (page 27), Chocolate and Burnt Almond, (page 31), and Ratafia (page 37) Ice Creams with fresh Mango Coulis (page 77), Chantilly Cream (page 76) and a dusting of Powdered Praline (page 27).

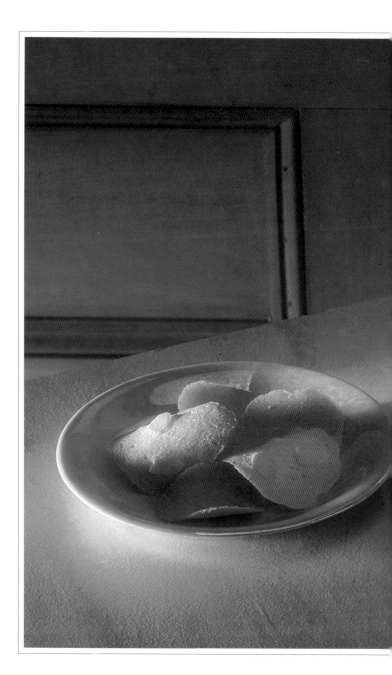

Left: Fatless Tuiles (page 72), centre: English Garden
with Redcurrant Fruit Coulis (page 77), right: Coupe Cassis with
Blackcurrant Fruit Coulis (page 77).

ICE CREAM BOMBES

Fancy ices were the height of fashion at the turn of the century. In The Complete Guide to the Art of Modern Cookery, *first published in 1902, the great chef Auguste Escoffier offers 77 recipes for ice cream bombes in a list that marches the length of the alphabet from Bombe Aboukir to Bombe Zamora by way of Bombes Frou-Frou, Hilda, Mathilde, Odette, Rosette and Tosca.*

A point to remember when constructing a bombe — usually in a tall metal dome, but a pudding basin will do — is to put the softest ice in the centre. This avoids a melting exterior with a rock hard core.

Parfaits (page 49) and many of the quick, still-frozen ices (pages 35-39) are suitable for bombe centres. Or there is the following classic basic bombe mousse which can be flavoured in numerous ways.

BASIC BOMBE MOUSSE

—————— SERVES 6 ——————

4 oz (110 g) granulated sugar
4 fl oz (110 ml) water
4 egg yolks
flavouring essence to taste

Put the sugar and water into a saucepan and heat gently until the sugar has dissolved completely. Wash down any sugar crystals from the sides of the pan with a pastry brush dipped in cold water. Raise the heat and boil the syrup, not too briskly, for about five minutes.

Put the egg yolks into a fairly large bowl and, whisking steadily, gradually add the syrup. Continue whisking until the mixture is thick and pale and about three times its original volume.

Set the bowl in cold water, or over ice, and whisk until the mousse is cold. Whisk in the flavouring. Cover and chill until needed. Keeps up to a week.

BOMBE ABOUKIR

This is the first of Escoffier's named bombes, a classic combination of pistachio ice cream and praline flavoured bombe mousse. Adjust the quantities of ice cream and bombe mousse to fit the mould, allowing a total of approximately 1¾ pints (1 litre) for 6 ample servings.

—————— SERVES 6 ——————

1 pint (560 ml) Cardamom and Pistachio Ice Cream (page 28)
1½ oz (40 g) blanched almonds
1½ oz (40g) caster sugar
4 fl oz (110 ml) double cream
½ pint (280 ml) Basic Bombe Mousse (left)

Chill the bombe mould well in the freezer. Ripen the pistachio ice cream in the refrigerator (page 5) until it is soft enough to be spooned. Line the mould with a layer of the pistachio ice cream, shaping it in an even layer right up to the rim. Cover the mould and freeze until the ice cream is firm again.

Use the almonds and sugar to make a praline as described on page 27, and grind the praline finely. Whip the cream until it holds soft peaks, then combine the bombe mousse, cream and powdered praline.

Spoon this mixture into the lined bombe mould, filling it completely. Cover and freeze until firm.

To serve the bombe, remove the lid and invert the mould on to a plate while it is still frozen hard. Wring out a cloth in hot water and use it to wrap the mould. Then holding the plate and mould together firmly, shake the bombe out of its container. Return the bombe to the freezer if not required immediately, or refrigerate it to ripen (page 5), as required, after smoothing over the surface if necessary and mopping up any drips.

Above: Bombe Aboukir.

ASSORTED BOMBES

The first bombes were frozen in spherical moulds and the name has stuck despite the move to dome-shaped ices and other variations.

Obviously there is no limit, except that of space, to the number of layers or flavours a bombe may have — which makes them a useful way to present ice cream leftovers elegantly.

Every cook will quickly find favourite combinations of flavours. But for any one in need of further inspiration, here is a description of the ices Escoffier named after all those girls.

Bombe Frou-Frou: Vanilla Ice Cream (page 24) filled with rum-flavoured Bombe Mousse (page 58) dotted with crystallized fruits.

Bombe Hilda: Hazelnut Ice Cream (page 27) filled with chartreuse-flavoured Bombe Mousse (page 58) containing Hazelnut Praline (page 27).

Bombe Mathilde: Kirsch-flavoured ice cream (Vanilla Ice Cream base, page 24, flavoured with 3 tablespoons kirsh), filled with apricot-flavoured Bombe Mousse (page 58). Use a strongly flavoured purée of dried apricots in place of half the usual quantity of cream.

Bombe Odette: Vanilla Ice Cream (page 24) filled with praline-flavoured Bombe Mousse (page 58).

Bombe Rosette: Vanilla Ice Cream (page 24) filled with Chantilly Cream (page 76) containing fresh redcurrants.

Bombe Tosca: Apricot Ice Cream (see the variation on Prune Ice Cream, page 42) filled with Maraschino-Flavoured Bombe Mousse (page 58) containing diced fruit.

Left: Bombe Rosette, right: Bombe Tosca

BOMBE ZAMORA

The final bombe in Escoffier's ice cream alphabet is lined with coffee ice cream and filled with orange curaçao-flavoured mousse. Alternative orange flavoured liqueurs include Grand Marnier and Cointreau.

―――――― SERVES 6 ――――――

1 pint (560 ml) Coffee Ice Cream (page 31)
4 fl oz (110 ml) double cream
3 tablespoons orange curaçao
½ pint (280 ml) Basic Bombe Mousse (page 58)

Chill the bombe mould well in the freezer. Ripen the coffee ice cream (page 5) until it is soft enough to be spooned. Line the mould with a layer of coffee ice cream keeping the thickness as even as possible right up to the rim. Cover and freeze until the ice cream is firm, again.

Whip the cream with the curaçao until it holds soft peaks then whisk it lightly into the bombe mousse. Spoon this mixture into the lined bombe mould, filling it completely. Cover and freeze it until firm.

To serve the bombe, remove the lid and invert the mould on to a plate while it is still frozen hard. Wring out a cloth in hot water and use it to wrap the mould. Then holding the plate and mould together firmly, shake the bombe out of its container. Return the bombe to the freezer if not required immediately, or refrigerate it to ripen (page 5), after smoothing over the surface if necessary and mopping up any drips.

BAKED ALASKA

Illustrated on page 67

Baked Alaska is one of the minor wonders of the world – ice cream straight from the oven in a coat of warm meringue appears to defy common sense. The trick, for so it appears, is that the thousands of tiny air bubbles in the meringue effectively insulate the ice cream for the short time it is in the oven.
Whatever flavour of ice cream you choose, freeze it in a brick-shaped mould. A plastic freezer box is ideal because it allows the ice cream to be unmoulded without dipping the container in hot water. Never ripen (page 5) ice cream when making Baked Alaska.
The sponge cake base should be about ½ in (1 cm) thick, the same shape as the ice cream brick and about ½ in (1 cm) wider all round. Use the Chocolate Sponge recipe on page 65, baking it on a Swiss roll tray and cutting it to fit. Alternatively, use any other plain sponge cake. The meringue may be the cooked Meringue Layer described on page 76, or the easy recipe below.

―――――― SERVES 6 ――――――

1 brick Cassata Ice Cream (page 24)
1 sponge cake base (follow recipe given for Chocolate Ice Cream Cake, page 65)
3 egg whites
3 oz (85 g) caster sugar

Heat the oven to 450°F (230°C, gas mark 8).

Place the cake base on a baking sheet and position the ice cream on top of it. Put them in the freezer while making the meringue.

Whisk the egg whites until they hold soft peaks, then whisk in the sugar, a little at a time, until the meringue is thick and glossy and holds firm peaks.

Spoon or pipe the meringue in an even layer over the top and sides of the ice cream and cover the sides of the cake as well.

Bake in the oven for about 5 minutes, to just brown the meringue lightly. Serve at once.

Above: Bombe Zamora.

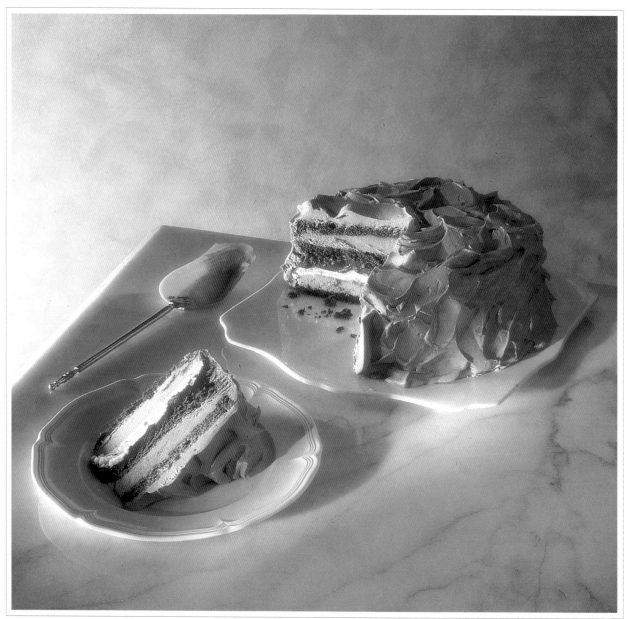

Above: Chocolate Ice Cream Cake.

CHOCOLATE ICE CREAM CAKE

Mostly ice cream and not too much cake is the right formula for ice cream cakes of any flavour. Rich ices that neither freeze too hard nor melt as soon as you look at them are the ones to choose for cake making.

———————— SERVES 20 ————————

for the cake
4 eggs
4 oz (120 g) caster sugar
3 oz (85 g) plain flour
1 oz (25 g) cocoa
1 teaspoon baking powder
1 × 12-in (30-cm) Meringue Layer (page 76)
for the filling
1¼ pints (750 ml) Chocolate Ice Cream (page 31)
1¼ pints (750 ml) Chazel Ice Cream (page 38)
1¼ pints (750 ml) Chocolate Marquise (see page 47)
for the decoration
¼ pint (150 ml) sweetened condensed milk
4 oz (110 g) dark chocolate, broken up
½ pint (280 ml) whipping cream

Heat the oven to 400°F (200°C, gas mark 6).

To make the cake, beat the eggs with the sugar until the mixture is pale and thick, and falls back leaving a trail when the beaters are lifted.

Sift together the flour, cocoa and baking powder and fold them into the egg mixture. Turn the mixture into a 12-in (30-cm) round spring-form cake tin lined with baking parchment and bake it for about 15 minutes or until a skewer inserted into the centre comes out clean.

Leave the cake to cool in its tin for 10 minutes before turning it on to a wire rack and stripping off the lining paper. When it is quite cold split it into 3 layers.

To assemble the cake, put the first sponge layer on a flat serving plate or base, checking first that the freezer door will shut behind it. Spread the cake with the chazel ice cream which has been partially frozen, or if made earlier, ripened to a spreadable consistency (page 5).

Top with the meringue and freeze until firm.

Spread a layer of partially frozen or softened chocolate marquise over the meringue and top with the second sponge layer. Freeze until firm.

Spread a layer of partially frozen or ripened chocolate ice cream over the sponge and top with the last sponge layer. Freeze until firm.

To make the frosting, heat the condensed milk and chocolate in a saucepan, stirring, until the chocolate has melted. Allow to cool, then chill in the refrigerator.

Whisk the chilled chocolate mixture vigorously to lighten it. Whip the cream until it holds soft peaks, then combine it with the chocolate mixture, whisking them together lightly.

Spread the top and sides of the cake with the chocolate cream. This can be finished in one of two ways: either pull it into frosted peaks using the tip of a rounded knife; or smooth it completely and comb it with wavy lines, using a clean coarse-toothed comb.

Freeze the cake just long enough to firm the icing, then cover it and freeze until firm.

STRAWBERRY ICE CREAM CAKE

Layers of meringue sandwiched with fresh Strawberry and Lemon Ice Creams make an ice cream cake that can be decorated at the last minute with fresh fruit.

———— SERVES 12 ————

4×9-in (22.5-cm) Meringue Layers (page 76)
1 recipe Strawberry Ice Cream (page 41)
1 recipe Lemon Ice Cream (page 35)
for the decoration
fresh strawberries

Place a meringue layer on a flat plate on which the cake can be frozen and later served. Spread it with half the partially frozen or ripened (page 5) strawberry ice cream and top with another meringue layer. Freeze until firm.

Spread with approximately one-third of the partially frozen or ripened lemon ice cream and top with another meringue layer. Freeze until firm.

To complete the assembly, spread the remaining strawberry ice cream over the meringue and top with the last meringue layer. Freeze until firm.

Finally ice the cake with the remaining lemon ice cream, giving it a smooth or peaked finish. A smoothly iced cake can be combed (see previous recipe) or decorated like a conventionally iced cake with slightly sweetened whipped double cream. Allow about 1 oz (25 g) icing sugar to every ¼ pint (150 ml) double cream. Because cream holds its shape less well than most icings, elaborate decorations are not advisable. Freeze the cake until firm before covering it for freezer storage. Decorate with strawberries.

Left: Baked Alaska,
right: Strawberry Ice Cream Cake.

Left: Carob Ice Cream, right: Honey Yoghurt Ice with delice biscuits.

HONEY YOGHURT ICE

Plain yoghurt sweetened with honey makes the simplest of ices. The richer the yoghurt and the sweeter the ice, the easier it is to achieve a smooth texture. So if using low-fat yoghurt and little honey 2 or 3 beatings may be required during freezing.

———————— SERVES 6 ————————

1¼ pints (560 ml) plain yoghurt
6 tablespoons strongly perfumed honey

Stir the honey into the yoghurt, adding more honey if the mixture is not sweet enough.

Freeze in a sorbetière following the manufacturer's instructions. Or still-freeze (page 4), vigorously whisking the partially frozen ice several times during the freezing process.

CAROB ICE CREAM

Carob powder is a useful substitute for cocoa in recipes where the taste of chocolate is wanted without the side effects experienced by some migraine sufferers and others sensitive to substances in cocoa. Carob powder is widely available in health food shops.

———————— SERVES 6 ————————

6 egg yolks
8 oz (225 g) soft light brown sugar
4 tablespoons carob powder
1¼ pints (700 ml) milk
vanilla extract to taste

Whisk the egg yolks with the sugar until pale and fluffy, then whisk in the carob powder. Gradually whisk in the milk.

Cook the custard, heating it gently in a heavy saucepan over a very low heat, or cook it in the top of a double boiler, stirring constantly until the custard is thick enough to coat the back of a wooden spoon.

Remove the custard from the heat and set it aside to cool, stirring it from time to time to prevent a skin forming. Then add vanilla extract to taste, remembering that the flavour will fade with freezing.

Freeze in a sorbetière following the manufacturer's instructions. Or still-freeze (page 4), vigorously whisking the partially frozen ice at least once during the freezing process.

STRAWBERRY SORBET

Ripe fruit has its own sugars which make it unnecessary, for taste reasons, to add more. Using a sorbetière which freezes and churns simultaneously, puréed soft fruits or freshly squeezed orange juice need only to be frozen to make acceptable sorbets. Without the help of sugar or a sorbetière to inhibit the formation of ice crystals, the addition of a little gelatine helps to smooth ices made by hand.

—— SERVES 6 ——

1 lb (450 g) ripe strawberries, hulled
½ pint (280 ml) fresh orange juice
1 tablespoon powdered gelatine
3 tablespoons water

Purée the strawberries by pressing them through a sieve, or by processing them lightly in a blender or food processor and straining the purée. Stir in the orange juice and set the mixture aside for about 2 hours to allow the flavour to develop.

Sprinkle the gelatine over the water in a small saucepan. Set it aside for a few minutes to swell and soften, then heat it gently, without allowing it to boil, stirring until the gelatine has dissolved completely. Allow it to cool a little, then stir the liquid gelatine into the fruit purée.

Freeze in a sorbetière following the manufacturer's instructions. Or still-freeze (page 4), vigorously whisking the partially frozen ice at least once during the freezing process.

VANILLA ICE

Low-fat, low-sugar ices need special care in the making if the result is to be pleasing. It is with these mixtures that a machine which whisks and freezes simultantously is such a boon. Frequent whisking to break down the size of the ice crystals is the answer when making this kind of ice by hand.

—— SERVES 6 ——

1¼ pints (700 ml) skimmed milk
1 vanilla pod, split lengthways
2 tablespoons cornflour
4 oz (110 g) soft light brown sugar
1 tablespoon powdered gelatine
3 tablespoons water

Put the milk and vanilla pod into a saucepan and bring to the boil. Immediately take off the heat, and set aside to cool. When it is quite cold, remove the vanilla pod which can be washed and dried and used again.

Mix the cornflour with the sugar and stir in a little of the milk to make a smooth paste. Reheat the remaining milk to boiling point and gradually stir it into the cornflour and sugar mixture. Return the custard to the pan and cook, stirring, until it has thickened. Simmer for 5 minutes, then take off the heat and leave to cool.

In the meantime, sprinkle the gelatine over the water in a small saucepan. Set it aside for a few minutes to swell and soften, then heat very gently without allowing it to boil, stirring until the gelatine has dissolved completely. Stir the liquid gelatine into the cool custard.

Freeze in a sorbetière following the manufacturer's instructions. Or still-freeze (page 4), vigorously whisking the partially frozen ice two or three times during the freezing process.

Top: Strawberry Sorbet, below: Vanilla Ice with Tuiles (page 72).

FATLESS TUILES

Illustrated on pages 74/75

Fragile biscuit baskets are attractive containers for ices. This fatless version of the classic recipe was evolved by Anton Mosimann for the style of cooking he has called cuisine naturelle. The same mixture can be rolled, while it is still warm and pliable, round the handle of a wooden spoon to make cigarette biscuits. Smaller tuiles can be moulded in a gentle curve over a rolling pin or shaped into cornets round cream horn moulds.

MAKES ABOUT 8 BASKETS

8 oz (225 g) icing sugar, sifted
8 oz (225 g) plain flour
6 large egg whites
a pinch of salt
finely grated zest of 3 oranges
2 oz (50 g) flaked almonds

Mix together the icing sugar, flour, egg whites and salt to make a thick, smooth batter. Strain the batter if necessary, to remove any lumps.

Add the orange zest and almonds and set the mixture aside for 2 hours.

Heat the oven to 350°F (180°C, gas mark 4).

Using your fingers, spread half the mixture into 4 rough 7-in (18-cm) circles on non-stick sheets. Bake for about 8 minutes, until golden.

Lift the biscuits from the trays one at a time and immediately drape each circle over a well-oiled inverted cup or small tumbler. The warm biscuits will droop into a rough basket shape. As the tuiles cool, they become firm and crisp. If any harden before they have been moulded, they can be softened again in the oven.

Bake and mould the remaining mixture in the same way.

Tuiles quickly become soggy when exposed to damp air, so as soon as they are quite cold, store them in an airtight tin.

CLASSIC TUILES

Illustrated on pages 74/75

This conventional recipe for tuiles contains butter. The newly baked biscuits can be moulded in the same ways as described in the previous recipe.

MAKES ABOUT 50

4 oz (120 g) butter, softened
4 oz (120 g) caster sugar
5 large egg whites
vanilla extract
4 oz (120 g) plain flour

Heat the oven to 400°F (200°C, gas mark 6).

Cream the butter in a mixing bowl, add the sugar and beat until the mixture is pale and fluffy. Beat in the egg whites, a little at a time, and a few drops of vanilla extract, then fold in the flour.

Pipe or spoon small mounds of the mixture on to well-greased baking sheets, spacing them well apart so that they have room to spread. Bake for about 10 minutes, or until they are pale gold in the centre and darker at the edges.

Cool the tuiles on a wire rack and as soon as they are quite cold, store them in an airtight tin.

BRANDY SNAP BASKETS

Illustrated on pages 74/75

Brandy snaps can be moulded into baskets, making crisp containers for creamy ices. Bake the snaps a few at a time and mould them while they are still hot from the oven over inverted cups or tumblers which have been well oiled or buttered.

—————————— MAKES ABOUT 6 ——————————

2 oz (50 g) butter
2 oz (50 g) granulated or caster sugar
2 tablespoons golden syrup or molasses
2 oz (50 g) plain flour
a pinch of salt
½ teaspoon ground ginger
1 teaspoon lemon juice
1 teaspoon brandy

Heat the oven to 325°F (160°C, gas mark 3) and line a baking sheet with baking parchment or buttered greaseproof paper.

Heat the butter, sugar and molasses in a small saucepan until the mixture is warm and melted but not hot. Sift together the flour, salt and ginger and stir them into the liquid butter mixture. Stir in the brandy and lemon juice.

Drop 2-tablespoonful blobs of batter, 4 at a time, on to the prepared baking sheet, spacing them well apart. Bake for 8-10 minutes, or until they are brown and bubbling.

Remove from the oven and allow the brandy snaps to cool on the tray for about 1 minute before lifting them, one at a time, and draping them over well-oiled inverted cups or tumblers. As the biscuits dry they become brittle and firm.

Bake and mould the remaining mixture in the same way.

SHORTCAKE THINS

Illustrated on pages 74/75

Melting shortcake biscuits eat well with any ice.

—————————— MAKES ABOUT 50 ——————————

3 oz (85 g) butter, softened
5 oz (140 g) caster sugar
1 egg yolk
finely grated zest of 1 lemon (optional)
6 oz (170 g) plain flour

Heat the oven to 350°F (180°C, gas mark 4).

Cream the butter in a mixing bowl, add the sugar and beat until the mixture is pale and fluffy. Beat in the egg yolk and lemon zest if used, then work in the flour and salt to make a stiff dough. Chill the dough in the refrigerator for about 30 minutes.

Roll out the dough to a thickness of about ³⁄₁₆ in (0.5 cm) and use plain or fancy cutters to stamp out the biscuits. Arrange them on greased and floured baking sheets and bake for about 10 minutes, or until pale gold.

Cool the biscuits on a wire rack and as soon as they are quite cold, store them in an airtight tin.

RATAFIAS

Ratafias, like tuiles, are a useful recipe for using up spare egg whites after making custard based ices. These old fashioned almond biscuits can be served with ices, or crushed and incorporated into them.

—————— **MAKES ABOUT 100** ——————

5 large egg whites
8 oz (225 g) ground almonds
12 oz (340 g) icing sugar
almond or ratafia essence

Heat the oven to 300°F (150°C, gas mark 2).

Whisk the egg whites until they hold stiff peaks, then fold in the ground almonds, sugar and essence to taste. Mix well to make a soft, sticky dough.

Pipe the mixture in small mounds (a teaspoonful or less) onto baking sheets lined with edible rice paper or non-stick baking parchment. Space the ratafias to allow a little spreading.

Bake for about 45 minutes, or until they are a pale, pinkish brown.

Leave the ratafias on the papers to cool on a wire rack. When they are quite cold, peel off the baking parchment, or trim the rice paper neatly round each ratafia.

Ratafias keep well for several weeks if stored in an airtight tin.

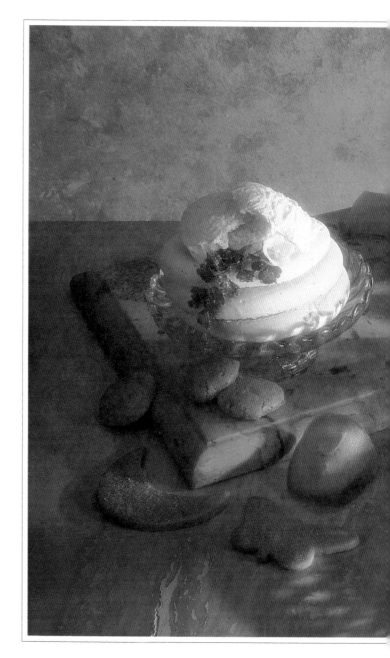

Clockwise, from top left: Meringue Basket (page 76), Fatless and Classic Tuiles (page 72), Brandy Snap Basket (page 73), Crystallized Flowers (page 78), Ice Cream with Mango Fruit Coulis (page 77), Shortcake Thins (page 73) and Ratafia Biscuits.

MERINGUE

Illustrated on pages 74/75

For meringue nests, and for layers that can be built into all manner of iced desserts, meringue made with hot sugar syrup gives better results than egg whites whisked with loose sugar. All types of meringue keep well once baked, but this one is quite stable before it is dried. It can be stored for several days in the refrigerator, and a spoonful or two used when needed to lighten a sorbet or whipped cream.
Copper bowls really do produce more and stronger meringue from fewer egg whites. The reason is a reaction between the metal and a component of egg. To maximize this effect always use a balloon whisk with a copper bowl. When using an electric whisk, use a narrow, straight-sided bowl, and in either case, make sure that the utensils are clean and dry, and that the egg whites are at room temperature.

MAKES 6 NESTS OR 2 9-in (23-cm) LAYERS

8 oz (225 g) granulated sugar
¼ pint (150 ml) water
4 egg whites

Put the sugar and water into a small saucepan and heat until the sugar has dissolved completely. Raise the heat and boil the syrup to the hard ball stage (about 250°F/ 121°C, on a sugar thermometer). To test without a thermometer, drop a little of the syrup into iced water then roll into a ball with your fingers. When the cold plunge firms the syrup sufficiently to roll it into a tough lump, it has reached the hard ball stage.

While the syrup is boiling, whisk the egg whites until they hold stiff peaks. Whisking continuously, gradually add the hot sugar syrup. Continue whisking until the meringue is cold.

To make meringue nests, line one or more baking sheets with baking parchment and mark on them 6 circles about 3½ in (9 cm) in diameter.

Heat the oven to 225°F (110°C, gas mark ¼).

Spoon large mounds of meringue on to the sheets, and use the back of the spoon to spread it into circles. Make a shallow depression on top of each mound.

Alternatively, fit a large piping bag with a plain nozzle at least ½ in (1.5 cm) in diameter. Fill the bag with meringue and pipe circular bases, filling in the outlines from the centre outwards. Then pipe two neat circles, one on top of the other, around the edge of the bases.

Bake the meringues in the oven for about 3 hours. Check from time to time, and if the meringues begin to colour, reduce the heat still further.

To make meringue layers, mark prepared baking sheets with 2 large circles about 9 in (23 cm) diameter. Pipe a single layer of meringue, filling each circle from the centre outwards. Alternatively, divide the meringue between the two outlines and spread it out evenly, using a spatula, to fill the circles.

Bake the layers at the same temperature as nests.

CHANTILLY CREAM

Lighter and sweeter than plain whipped cream, a froth of chantilly cream is a classic topping. It can be flavoured with a few drops of vanilla extract, or a liqueur may be substituted for all or part of the water.

MAKES ABOUT 1 PINT (560 ml)

3 tablespoons water or liqueur
½ pint (280 ml) double cream, chilled
1 tablespoon caster sugar
real vanilla extract (optional)

Put the water (or liqueur) into a bowl and chill in the freezer until ice crystals begin to form. Chill the beaters or whisk as well.

Add the cream and whisk until the mixture holds soft peaks. Sprinkle on the sugar and a dash of vanilla, if used, and whisk it in lightly.

Use to decorate ices, coupes or sundaes.

SOFT FRUIT COULIS

Illustrated on pages 56/57

Fresh sauces made with ripe soft fruits complement many ices. Raspberry coulis is the chefs' favourite. Strawberry and Mango are also especially good, but any other soft fruit, from peaches to kiwis, can be called upon.
Blackberries, blueberries and blackcurrants all make dramatically dark sauces, and the colour and flavour of all three fruits is the better for being lightly cooked. In each case, sweat the fruit in a covered pan over a low heat until the juices begin to run before puréeing it.
I find that I use less and less sugar in fresh fruit sauces – just enough to bring out the best of the flavour. In fact the sugar is here used as a seasoning only.

MAKES ABOUT 1 PINT (560 ml)

1 lb (450 g) ripe raspberries, fresh or frozen and thawed
about 4 tablespoons icing sugar
lemon juice to taste

Purée the raspberries by pressing them through a fine sieve, or by processing them briefly in a blender or food processor then sieving them to remove the pips.

Stir in the icing sugar and lemon juice to taste, then set the sauce aside for 1 hour, to allow the flavour to develop. Serve chilled.

HOT CHOCOLATE SAUCE

A glossy dark chocolate sauce, that does not harden in contact with ice cream, is an essential addition to every cook's repertoire.

MAKES ABOUT ½ PINT (280 ML)

4 oz (120 g) dark chocolate
4 fl oz (110 ml) golden syrup or honey
2 tablespoons any liqueur (optional)

Break the chocolate into a bowl or the top of a double boiler. Add the syrup or honey and liqueur and stir over simmering water until melted, to make a smooth, hot sauce.

CHOCOLATE FUDGE SAUCE

Condensed milk and plain chocolate make an easy and irresistible hot fudge sauce.

MAKES ABOUT ½ PINT (280 ML)

2 oz (50 g) dark chocolate
4 fl oz (120 ml) sweetened condensed milk
4 tablespoons fresh milk
1 oz (25 g) unsalted butter

Break the chocolate into a bowl or the top of a double boiler. Add the condensed milk and heat over simmering water, stirring until the chocolate has melted and the sauce is smooth. Beat in the milk, followed by the butter. Serve hot.

CRYSTALLIZED FLOWERS

Illustrated on pages 74/75

There is no comparison between the brash colour and coarse texture of commercially crystallized flowers – usually violets and roses – and the delicacy of petals frosted at home. It is the simplest of procedures and once done, the flowers will keep for as long as a year.
There are no prettier or more appropriate decorations for ices than fragile, scented, sugared flowers. Not all flowers are edible, of course, but all in the following list are safe: primroses, violets, apple blossom, wallflowers, marigolds, nasturtiums, geraniums, pinks, carnations, roses, jasmine, lilac, borage, orange blossom, and freesias. Check the safety of any flowers not listed.
And all the culinary herbs can be crystallized too, of course.

────────── **50 PETALS OR FLOWERS** ──────────

Fresh, dry flowers in perfect condition – petals or small flowers
1 egg white
8 oz (225 g) caster sugar

If you are crystallizing roses, or any other large flowers, separate them into petals. In the case of roses, nip off the white heel at the base of each petal. Very small flowers, individual lilac blossoms, violets and primroses, can be left whole.

Put the egg white into a saucer and break it up a little with a fork.

Spread some of the sugar on a plate and put some more into a small sieve.

Using a small, soft brush, paint each petal or flower lightly all over with egg white. Lay the petals or flowers on the plate of sugar and sprinkle more sugar over them. The sugar sticks best to freshly painted petals, so coat and sugar them one at a time.

Lay the flowers on baking sheets lined with paper and dry them in a barely warm oven or airing cupboard, for 24 hours or until they are dry and brittle. Turn the flowers several times in the first few hours of drying.

The colour of the flowers is preserved remarkably well by this method. Once crystallized, flowers should be stored in airtight containers away from bright light.

BASIC SORBET SYRUP

For almost instant ices, basic sorbet syrup is a useful standby. It keeps for several weeks in the refrigerator, ready to combine at a moment's notice with fruit purée or juice and perhaps a liqueur.

────────── **MAKES ABOUT 3 PINTS (1.7 LITRES)** ──────────

1½ lb (675 g) granulated sugar
1¾ pints (1 litre) boiling water

Pour the boiling water over the sugar and stir until it has dissolved completely. Cool and store, covered, until needed.

INDEX